PANZERFAUST
VS
SHERMAN

European Theater 1944–45

STEVEN J. ZALOGA

OSPREY PUBLISHING
Bloomsbury Publishing Plc
PO Box 883, Oxford, OX1 9PL, UK
1385 Broadway, 5th Floor, New York, NY 10018, USA
E-mail: info@ospreypublishing.com
www.ospreypublishing.com

OSPREY is a trademark of Osprey Publishing Ltd

First published in Great Britain in 2019

A catalog record for this book is available from the British Library.

ISBN: PB 9781472832313; eBook 9781472832320;
ePDF 9781472832306; XML 9781472832337

19 20 21 22 23   10 9 8 7 6 5 4 3 2 1

Maps by www.bounford.com
Index by Rob Munro
Typeset by PDQ Digital Media Solutions, Bungay, UK
Printed in China by Toppan Leefung Printing Ltd.

Osprey Publishing supports the Woodland Trust, the UK's leading woodland
conservation charity.

To find out more about our authors and books visit
www.ospreypublishing.com. Here you will find extracts, author interviews,
details of forthcoming events and the option to sign up for our newsletter.

Author's note

All photos, unless otherwise credited, are from official US government sources
including NARA (National Archives and Records Administration), College
Park, MD; the Patton Museum formerly at Fort Knox, KY; and the Ordnance
Museum formerly at Aberdeen Proving Ground, MD.

Editor's note

All measurements are given in US customary with the exception of armor
thickness, which is given in millimeters, and weapons calibers, which are given
in US customary or metric depending on the weapon's origins.

Title-page photograph: The various US field armies had different policies on
expedient armor. When the 14th Armored Division was transferred from the
Seventh US Army (SUSA) to Gen. George S. Patton's Third US Army
(TUSA) on April 23, 1945, there was some dispute over the matter. Here,
Patton is depicted moments after berating the crew of an M4A3E8 of the
14th Armored Division for the sandbag armor on their tank.

Glossary

AFV	armored fighting vehicle
CCA	Combat Command A
FPZ	*Faustpatrone Zünder* (*Panzerfaust* impact fuze)
FUSA	First US Army
GMC	Gun Motor Carriage
HASAG	Hugo Schneider Aktien-Gesellschaft, Leipzig
HH.3	Magnetische Hafthohlladung 3kg (magnetic hand-emplaced shaped charge)
KG	*Kampfgruppe* (battlegroup)
KStN	*Kriegsstärkenachweisungen* (war establishment strength)
lFH	*leichte Feldhaubitze* (light field howitzer)
NUSA	Ninth US Army
OKH	Oberkommando des Heeres (Army High Command)
PaK	*Panzerabwehr-Kanone* (antitank gun)
Panzerjäger	tank destroyer
PzKpfw	*Panzerkampfwagen* (tank)
RM	Reichsmark
RPzB 54	Raketenpanzerbüchse 54 (rocket antitank rifle)
sFH	*schwere Feldhaubitze* (heavy field howitzer)
SUSA	Seventh US Army
TF	Task Force
TUSA	Third US Army
USAAF	United States Army Air Forces
WASAG	Westfälisch-Anhaltische-Sprengstoff-Aktien-Gesellschaft, Reinsdorf
Wehrmacht	German armed forces

Key to military symbols

CONTENTS

Introduction	4
Chronology	8
Design and Development	10
Technical Specifications	40
The Combatants	51
The Strategic Situation	60
Combat	64
Analysis	71
Aftermath	76
Further Reading	78
Index	80

INTRODUCTION

This book examines the impact of the revolutionary new antitank weapons introduced on the battlefield in late 1943. The focus of this book is the confrontation between the German *Panzerfaust* and similar weapons such as the *Panzerschreck* against US Army M4 medium tanks in the European Theater of Operations (ETO) in 1944–45.

At the outset of World War II, there was considerable controversy about the types of weapons needed by the infantry to defend against tanks. During World War I, the only dedicated infantry antitank weapons were antitank rifles. Through the late 1930s,

A comparison of three of the German shaped-charge antitank launchers at a display at the Russian Military Historical Museum of Artillery, Engineers and Signal Corps in St. Petersburg. On the left is the original RPzB 54, in the center a Panzerfaust 60, and on the right is the shorter RPzB 54/1.

most tanks were armored to much the same level as World War I tanks – usually about 15mm thick, which was enough to protect against common infantry weapons such as rifles and light machine guns. While antitank rifles could penetrate such tank armor, their rounds typically lacked sufficient energy after penetration to cause much damage inside the tank.

To damage a tank sufficiently, a larger weapon was needed. This typically took the form of an antitank gun in the 25–37mm range. These weapons were significantly heavier and more expensive than typical infantry weapons, and so were deployed in small numbers. Technically, the new antitank guns were a major threat to the tank. Tactically, however, they posed a much more modest threat since they were seldom available in sufficient numbers to stop a concentrated tank attack.

With the combat debut of dedicated infantry antitank guns during the Spanish Civil War of 1936–39, tank advocates suddenly realized that the existing levels of tank armor were wholly inadequate. As a result, a new arms race began to increase tank armor to 30mm thick or more. Gradually tanks began to appear with armor thick enough to resist typical 37mm antitank guns. This became very apparent during the Battle of France in May–June 1940 with the debut of more heavily armored tank types such as the French and British infantry tanks that had armor 40mm thick or more. Yet the campaign was over so quickly that the Wehrmacht became complacent. A new 5cm antitank gun, the PaK 38, was slowly entering service, but the Wehrmacht continued to rely on the much less powerful 3.7cm PaK 36 antitank gun.

In the summer of 1941 during Operation *Barbarossa*, the invasion of the Soviet Union, the Wehrmacht was confronted by even more heavily armored Soviet tanks, namely the T-34 medium tank and the KV heavy tank. In most circumstances, these tanks were impervious to both the older PaK 36 – derisively nicknamed "the door knocker" since all it could do was announce its presence to its Soviet opponents – and the new PaK 38. Soviet tanks literally drove over German PaK 36 with impunity.

While new German antitank guns emerged in 1942, such as the 7.5cm PaK 40, the German infantry endured more than a year of combat during which they had few weapons capable of dealing with the Soviet tank threat. Until the new and more powerful antitank guns appeared, the German infantry had to rely on weapons of desperation. Hand-grenade warheads were bundled together in a cluster in the hope of creating an explosive force powerful enough to damage a Soviet tank; they were

The *Panzerfaust* was classified as a munition rather than as a weapon in the Wehrmacht, and so there was no specific number assigned to German tables of organization and equipment. They were issued in increasingly large numbers in early 1945 once production ramped up to over 1 million rounds per month in November 1944. This is a Panzerfaust 30 (gross) in the hands of a young German soldier on the Eastern Front in February 1945.

One of the more effective expedient armor packages was developed by the Ninth US Army (NUSA) and consisted of a base layer of steel track blocks, followed by sandbags, and finally a cover of camouflage net to keep the sandbags in place. This is an example of expedient armor on an M4A3 of Co. H, 67th Armored Regiment, 2d Armored Division in Priesterath, Germany, on February 28, 1945, while on the way to the Rhine River.

nearly useless. Molotov cocktails were issued; but the Red Army had already witnessed their effects in Spain and all new tank designs were protected against gasoline weapons. One of the few effective weapons was the Teller antitank mine. German infantry, displaying immense courage, would sneak up to a Soviet tank, and plant the mine under its tracks. Many brave German soldiers died trying to knock out Soviet tanks with slapdash antitank improvisations.

Traditional methods of antitank warfare relied on kinetic energy to penetrate tank armor; but it took a very large projectile, fired with a great deal of propellant, from a very large gun to penetrate 90mm of steel armor. Infantry antitank guns became so large and heavy that they had to be moved by vehicle, preferably cross-country half-tracks, rather than by a few infantrymen like the old but mobile 3.7cm PaK 36 or its Allied equivalents. Owing to their size and weight, these large antitank guns were available in very limited numbers. In a 1943 German infantry division, for example, there were only 12 7.5cm antitank guns, guarding a front many miles wide. When one antitank gun faced one tank, it was an even match. When one antitank gun faced a platoon of five tanks, however, it might knock out one or two tanks before it was destroyed by the other tanks. Tanks were invariably more mobile than antitank guns, and so could concentrate their numbers against weak points in the defense.

The important breakthrough in antitank technology during 1942 was the application of shaped-charge technology to the antitank fight. Shaped charges stemmed from the earlier hollow-charge phenomenon. Engineers had known for some time that when a high-explosive charge was detonated around a cavity, the blast could be focused by the cavity to enhance the damage. German paratroopers used hollow-charge demolition munitions in the May 1940 attacks on Belgian fortresses. Shaped charges were a type of hollow charge that added an important ingredient: a metal liner between the warhead's explosive and the cavity. When the warhead was detonated, the explosive blast was focused on the metal liner, compressing it into a hypersonic stream of metal particles that could penetrate a great deal of steel armor.

The earliest shaped-charge antitank devices were still weapons of desperation. The Wehrmacht, for example, fielded a variety of hand-emplaced or hand-thrown weapons using shaped-charge warheads. These were dangerous to use and had a very low success rate, for few infantrymen had the courage to run up to a tank and place a charge against its hull armor. Many soldiers who tried to use these weapons died in the process. Clearly, a weapon was needed that would make it possible for the ordinary infantryman to combat a tank, preferably from the safety of distance. In 1942–43, several armies developed weapons that projected shaped-charge munitions against tanks. This book examines the confrontation between German shaped-charge weapons such as the *Panzerfaust* and *Panzerschreck* and US Army M4 medium tanks in the European Theater of Operations (ETO) during 1944–45.

SUSA in Alsace began fitting steel cages for sandbag armor on its tanks starting in January 1945. This is an early example of a tank so adapted from the 14th Armored Division with the cages only on the hull sides and not yet fitted to the turret. The tank is shown here in Niederbetschdorf, Alsace, on January 19, 1945.

CHRONOLOGY

1941
June 22 Operation *Barbarossa*, the German invasion of the Soviet Union, begins.

1942
March 9 The Panzervernichtungsabzeichen (Tank Destruction Badge) decoration is introduced in Germany.

April *Faustpatrone* and *Puppchen* development commences in Germany.

May Germany's HH.3 magnetic hand-emplaced shaped charge makes its debut on the Eastern Front.

1943
January HASAG begins development of the RPzB 54 launcher.

March Competitive trials of the *Faustpatrone* and RPzB 54 are undertaken at the Kummersdorf proving ground, Germany.

August *Faustpatrone* serial production begins.

October RPzB 54 serial production begins.

October The *Faustpatrone* sees its first widespread combat use on the Eastern Front.

October The Flintkote Company receives a US Army contract to develop plastic armor for tanks.

October 5 The first RPzB 54 deliveries are made.

November Hitler renames the *Faustpatrone* the *Panzerfaust*; the RPzB 54 becomes the *Panzerschreck*.

November The first *Puppchen* deliveries are made.

December 18 The Panzervernichtungsabzeichen decoration is expanded to include *Panzerschreck* gunners.

1944
January A protective shield is introduced on new-production *Panzerschreck* launchers.

February *Puppchen* production is canceled.

June 6 The D-Day landings begin in Normandy.

June 29–30 The battle of Villiers-Fossard takes place in Normandy.

July 18–24 Units of the First US Army begin to add expedient sandbag armor to their tanks as counter-*Panzerfaust* protection.

To attach concrete armor to their tanks, the 12th Armored Division maintenance crews first welded bolts to the armor, and then fastened two layers of steel mesh at 2in (51mm) intervals before finally welding a matrix of steel rebar to connect the bolts. This M4A3E8 is undergoing the expedient concrete armor upgrade carried out by the 134th Armored Ordnance Maintenance Battalion near Marlenheim, Alsace, on January 30, 1945.

July 25	Operation *Cobra*, the Allied breakout from Normandy, begins.
July 25	The 3d Armored Group conducts tests of sandbag armor in Normandy.
July 28	The 3d Armored Group tests expedient side armor using jerrycans filled with sand.
August 8	The US Army in Europe queries Ordnance about possible protection against shaped-charge ammunition.
November	Panzerfaust 100 production begins; *Panzerfaust* production reaches 1 million per month.
December	The Ninth US Army begins to fit its tanks with layered expedient armor.
December 3	HASAG tests *Panzerfäuste* against various antitank skirts.
December 20	RPzB 54/1 production is approved.

The RPzB 54/1 (left) is compared to a US Army M1A1 2.36in bazooka after its capture in Germany in early 1945.

1945

January 2	The 1st Armored Group tests "bazooka skirts" against *Panzerschreck* strikes.
January 31	The Seventh US Army begins adding expedient sandbag armor to its tanks.
February	The Third US Army begins to add extra layers of armor to its tanks.
February	The First Canadian Army experiments with counter-*Panzerfaust* techniques.
March	The 3d Armored Division adds steel armor to its tanks at a captured factory in Cologne.
April	The Soviet 5th Shock Army adopts counter-*Panzerfaust* screens for its tanks.

The *Panzerfaust* was aimed using a folding leaf sight in conjunction with a small pip at the top of the warhead. The sight had three range options (30m, 60m, and 80m) which prompted the gunner to raise or lower the elevation of the launch tube. This is a Panzerfaust 30 (gross) in the hands of a Finnish Army soldier in the summer of 1944. (SA-kuva)

DESIGN AND DEVELOPMENT

GERMAN SHAPED-CHARGE ANTITANK WEAPONS

As in most armed forces of the Blitzkrieg era, the Wehrmacht relied principally on antitank guns for defense against enemy tanks. In 1939, the principal type was the 3.7cm PaK 36, which was very effective against the lightly armored tanks of the late 1930s. The tank fighting in the Spanish Civil War in 1936–39 clearly demonstrated the vulnerability of lightly armored tanks such as the German PzKpfw I and Soviet T-26 to such weapons, which led some foreign military observers to conclude that antitank guns would sweep the battlefield of tanks in much the same way as the machine gun had swept the battlefield of cavalry in World War I.

Aside from the technical issue of armor penetration, the tactical issue of antitank gun density also became evident in the 1939–40 battles of World War II. Antitank guns were not available in sufficient numbers to defeat a concentrated tank attack. In the Wehrmacht of 1940, each infantry regiment had an antitank company (*Panzerabwehr-Kompanie*) with 12 3.7cm PaK 36 guns, and the division had an antitank battalion. The regimental frontage was typically 1km (1,094yd) or more wide, so the antitank guns tended to be scattered very thinly along the forward edge of battle. As a result, an enemy tank attack would encounter only a handful of antitank guns that could be quickly overwhelmed.

This problem was appreciated before the outbreak of World War II, and attempts were made to thicken the infantry's defenses by the addition of smaller and lighter antitank weapons. At the start of the war, German infantry regiments typically had an authorized strength of 27 antitank rifles. Most German infantry commanders realized that the antitank rifle was a marginal weapon at best, however, their use in 1918 during the later stages of World War I having proved very disappointing. Although the newer types of antitank rifles were lighter and more effective than the World War I types, they could only penetrate lightly armored tanks. More critically, their projectiles were so small that they could only damage an enemy tank and had very little chance of knocking out a tank.

The issue of infantry antitank defense became a crisis in the summer of 1941, when the Wehrmacht was confronted by large numbers of the new Soviet T-34 medium and KV heavy tanks. These thickly armored vehicles were completely impervious to the 3.7cm PaK 36 antitank gun. Even the new 5cm PaK 38 antitank gun had only marginal capabilities against these steel monsters at very close ranges from the side. There were a number of occasions in the summer of 1941 when German infantry units were routed by Soviet tank attacks, and German commanders cited numerous examples of "tank panic" along the front. The immediate solution was a heavier antitank gun, the 7.5cm PaK 40, but this did not appear until late 1942. Furthermore, it suffered the usual problem of being available in too small a number to provide an adequate level of antitank defense along an extended front line. Clearly some form of smaller, lighter, more numerous weapon was urgently needed to stengthen the infantry defenses.

EARLY SHAPED-CHARGE WEAPONS

Some form of gun relying on kinetic energy was out of the question simply due to the weight of a cannon powerful enough to penetrate armor more than 60mm thick. A more promising direction was the chemical energy warhead, specifically hollow charges, because a relatively small and lightweight hollow charge could penetrate a substantial amount of armor. The principle of shaped charges was known to engineers before World War II, but its application to weapon warheads took time. German *Fallschirmjäger* (airborne troops) used hollow charges in the attack on the Belgian Army's Fort Eben-Emael in 1940. This was an early and primitive type of hollow charge developed by a Dr. Wülfken, of the Heereswaffenamt (HWA: Army Ordnance Department). Unlike the later and improved shaped-charge warhead, these early hollow charges lacked a metal warhead liner. By adding a metal liner between the explosives and the cavity, however, the degree of penetration could be substantially increased. The detonation of the explosives around a cavity rapidly deformed the metal liner into a hypersonic stream of metal particles that had substantially better penetration than could be achieved by the hollow charge by itself. The pioneer of shaped-charge warheads in Germany during the war was an Austrian designer, Franz Rudolf Thomanek, working for one of the Luftwaffe research centers.

The initial application of the shaped-charge principle for German infantry antitank defense was in the form of a hand-emplaced grenade. The most successful of these was the Magnetische Hafthohlladung 3kg (HH.3: 3kg (6.6lb) magnetic hand-emplaced shaped charge). This grenade had a shaped-charge warhead with a

The Magnetische Hafthohlladung 3kg (HH 3: 3kg (6.6lb) magnetic hand-emplaced shaped charge) was the most successful of Germany's early shaped-charge antitank weapons. It was fastened to an enemy tank using the set of three strong magnets located in front of the conical warhead. This HH.3 was captured by the US Army in Tunisia in 1943 and is missing the detonation knob at the top of the handle.

FAR RIGHT

A preserved example of the HH.3 with arming plug. To encourage German infantry to employ these risky close-attack weapons, on March 9, 1942 the Oberkommando des Heeres (OKH: Army High Command) established the Panzervernichtungsabzeichen (Tank Destruction Badge), more formally called the Sonderabzeichen für das Niederkämpfen von Panzerkampfwagen durch Einzelkämpfer (Special Award for Close Combat against Tank by a Single Warrior). The award was limited to soldiers using close-combat devices, and excluded crew-served weapons such as antitank guns. The badge, worn on the right sleeve, was awarded for every tank knocked out. On December 18, 1943, the OKH expanded the award with a new gold badge to acknowledge the destruction of five enemy tanks. Through May 1944, about 10,000 of these badges had been awarded. The majority of these actions against enemy tanks involved use of the HH.3, but no detailed statistics appear to have been kept.

160mm diameter. At the front of the grenade was a set of three strong magnets. The infantryman would surreptitiously approach an enemy tank, attach the grenade to the armor using the magnets and then pull the detonation knob. The fuze had a 4.5–7-second delay to enable the infantryman to run away from the tank. On detonation, the HH.3 could penetrate about 130mm of armor – enough to penetrate most T-34 and KV armor. Not only could a shaped charge penetrate a substantial amount of armor, but also the penetrating jet sprayed the interior of the tank with incandescent metal spall, usually causing catastrophic damage and setting any combustible materials ablaze.

Production of the HH.3 began in 1942 and it first appeared on the Eastern Front in May that year. Only about 8,500 of these hand-emplaced grenades were produced in 1942, but the weapon proved so effective that by 1943 production increased to 358,400. Production ended in October 1944 with some 547,000 HH.3 having been manufactured.

The main problem with the HH.3 was that it required heroic bravery on the part of the infantryman tasked with attaching the grenade for its effective employment. It was more a weapon of desperation than an effective solution to the tank threat. Some other method of delivery was needed. One solution was the Panzerwurfmine-1 (leichte) (thrown tank mine-1 (light)), which resembled a conventional German stick hand-grenade but was larger and heavier with a 114mm warhead. When this hand-thrown antitank grenade was about to be thrown, the infantryman would remove the metal cap from the end of the grenade. In flight, a set of spring-actuated cloth fins on the tail section popped out to stabilize the grenade's direction of travel. On striking the tank, an impact fuze detonated the shaped-charge warhead. The Panzerwurfmine-1 did not appear until 1943, however, by which time more effective shaped-charge weapons were appearing.

The HWA worked on a variety of methods to launch shaped-charge warheads as alternatives to hand grenades. One of the first attempts was the Gewehrgranate zur Panzerbekämpfung Modell 1940 (rifle grenade antitank model 1940) developed by

The Panzerwurfmine-1 (leichte) (thrown tank mine-1 (light)) was a 1943 attempt to deploy a shaped-charge antitank weapon that could be thrown rather than hand-emplaced. It was quickly overshadowed by the far more practical *Panzerfaust*. This example was captured by the US Army during the fighting on the Cotentin Peninsula near Cherbourg in June 1944.

WASAG. Obsolete 7.92mm Panzerbüchse 39 antitank rifles were converted into grenade launchers by shortening their barrels and adding a grenade-launching cup. Although the grenade had a nominal penetration of 70mm of armor, the weapon was heavy and not especially effective in view of its very small warhead. It was largely withdrawn from service by 1943 due to its uninspiring performance on the battlefield.

THE *PUPPCHEN* AND *PANZERSCHRECK*

In early 1942, WASAG was given a contract by the HWA to develop an 8.8cm rocket-propelled shaped-charge projectile for the new *Raketenpanzerbüchse* (rocket antitank rifle), codenamed *Puppchen* (Little Doll). The *Puppchen* resembled a very small artillery piece with a conventional breech, but it weighed only about one-fifth as much as the obsolete 3.7cm PaK 36 antitank gun. The Raketenpanzerbüchse-Granate 4312 (RPzBGr 4312: antitank rocket projectile 4312) was loaded from the breech end like a conventional gun. When fired, a percussion cap ignited the rocket motor. The rocket was stabilized in flight by fins on the tail section, contained within a drum that centered the projectile as it moved down the barrel.

While the RPzBGr 4312 was under development, the Wehrmacht captured examples of the US Army's new 2.36in M1 antitank rocket launcher (commonly known as the "bazooka"), in Tunisia. The main innovation of this weapon was that the rocket was launched from a very simple, lightweight tube that was far less cumbersome than the *Puppchen*. Instead of using a percussion detonator, it used a simpler electrical detonator. As a result of this discovery, in January 1943 HASAG was given a contract to develop a suitable launcher, initially called the Schulder 75, while WASAG was

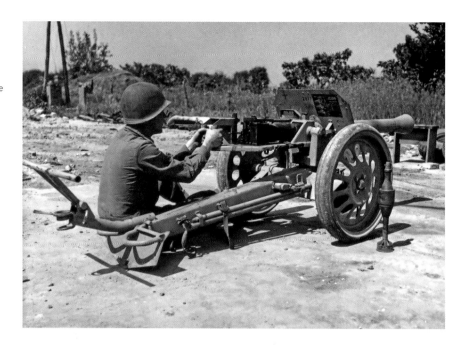

The *Raketenpanzerbüchse* (rocket antitank rifle), codenamed *Puppchen* (Little Doll), was the first of the rocket-launched antitank shaped-charge weapons. The rocket was loaded into the rear breech like a conventional artillery weapon. Although considerably lighter than existing antitank guns, the *Puppchen* was quickly overshadowed by the more versatile *Panzerschreck* (Tank Terror). This *Puppchen* was captured by the US Army near Anzio in Italy in the spring of 1944.

instructed to adapt the RPzBGr 4312 for tube launch by electrical ignition as the RPzBGr 4322. The new weapon received various names, being called variously the 8.8cm Raketenpanzerbüchse 54 (RPzB 54), or by its internal industrial name of Gerät 6030 Erntekranz (Harvest Wreath). Not surprisingly, it was dubbed the *Ofenrohr* (stove pipe) during development, and this name became semiofficial in production documents. In November 1943, Hitler authorized the official name *Panzerschreck* (Tank Terror) for the weapon.

Though the warhead section on both the *Panzerschreck*'s RPzBGr 4322 rocket projectile and the *Puppchen*'s RPzBGr 4312 were essentially identical, the rockets differed from one another in several respects. The *Puppchen* rocket was ignited by a mechanical firing pin striking a percussion cap in the tail of the rocket; the *Panzerschreck* rocket was electrically ignited like the US bazooka. The *Puppchen* used a smaller rocket engine charge due to its launch mode; but even though the *Puppchen*'s rocket contained less propellant, it had a greater effective range than the *Panzerschreck*:

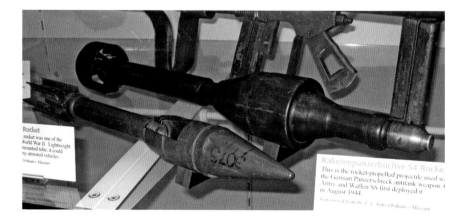

The 8.8cm *Panzerschreck* RPzBGr 4322 rocket was significantly larger than its US counterpart, the 2.36in M6A1 rocket shown here in front of it.

230m (252yd) against tanks and 700m (766yd) against bunkers or other non-armored targets. In contrast, the *Panzerschreck* had a maximum effective range of 150m (164yd) in its initial versions, and 200m (219yd) in the later production rockets, since much of its rocket exhaust was expended backward to make the weapon recoilless.

The original 1943 production series of the RPzB 54 launcher required the operator to wear a gas mask and protective clothing to protect against burns from the rocket exhaust. This is an RPzB 54 in use on the Eastern Front in February 1944.

By the time production of the two weapons was ready to start in late 1943, priority had generally shifted from the *Puppchen* to the *Panzerschreck*, which was viewed as a more versatile and efficient weapon. The plan was to begin production in September 1943 with 500 *Panzerschreck* launchers and 5,000 rockets, but lingering problems with the erratic performance of the warhead's impact fuze and the poor performance of the rocket propellant under extreme cold led to production delays. The first production batches of the rockets demonstrated numerous problems, delaying serial production until October 1943.

The first production batch of *Puppchen* launchers totaled 2,863 in 1943 and 288 in early 1944. A second production batch of 3,000 was canceled in February 1944. A total of 420,000 rockets for the *Puppchen* were ordered with deliveries starting in November 1943. The first batch of RPzBGr 4312 rockets were not delivered to the troops until February–March 1944. In the event, only 303,000 rockets were manufactured through July 1944 when production ended.

The HWA recognized that the *Panzerschreck* had a variety of technical problems, but it was placed into serial production anyway due to the urgency of the

To avoid the need for protective clothing for the *Panzerschreck* gunner, a shield was introduced in early 1944. This is a *Panzerschreck* in Finnish Army use in the summer of 1944. (SA-kuva)

requirement. The original production batches of 15,000 rockets were reliable only down to -10°C (14°F), which was certainly not suitable for Russian winters. As a result, these rockets generally were restricted to training use. To rush the weapon into service, the HWA decided to issue special *Wintermunition* ("winterized" rockets) which used a different propellant formulation to operate reliably down to -40°C (-40°F). These rockets were marked "Arkt" (Arctic) on the first batches issued in the winter of 1943–44, and "Arkt 44–45" the following winter; but they did not offer ideal operational characteristics in warm summer weather, so rockets with the normal, more efficient propellant were issued in the spring–summer of 1944. Another problem with the rocket was the irregular burn time of the rocket motor, which sometimes continued to burn for a few yards after the rocket left the launch tube, spraying the gunner with incandescent rocket debris. Efforts were made to develop a faster and more even-burning propellant, but this was not ready in early 1944.

At first, *Panzerschreck* crews were issued with gas masks and other protective clothing to protect them during the rocket launch. Eventually, a shield was developed, fitted with a small transparent mica window. The shield was gradually added on the production line in January–February 1944 as parts became available. A modification kit was also manufactured and dispatched to units already equipped with the *Panzerschreck* so that the weapon could be brought up to current standards. The shield and other upgrades increased the weight of the *Panzerschreck* from 21lb to 24lb. A total of 256,500 *Panzerschreck* launchers were ordered through July 1944, with production largely ending by August 1944.

The next stage of development was an improved rocket projectile, the RPzBGr 4992 Kurzbrenner (short burn). The rocket motor burned out completely before exiting the launch tube, providing better accuracy and decreasing the threat

RPzB 54 VARIANTS

This illustration shows the 1943-production RPzB 54 without shield (**1**) and the standard-production version (**2**) plus the RPzBGr 4322 rocket (**3**).

RPzB 54 TECHNICAL DATA

Caliber: 8.8cm
Length: 65in
Weight: 24lb
Muzzle velocity: 361ft/sec
Range: 150m (164yd)
Rocket weight: 7.2lb
Rocket length: 650mm (25.6in)
Warhead explosive: 23oz Cyclotol
Penetration: 160mm

of rocket debris injuring the gunner when fired. In addition, it boosted the rocket's maximum effective range from 150m (164yd) to 200m (219yd). The new rocket could be used with the original RPzB 54 launchers if they were modified with new sights. The new rocket also permitted the development of the handier RPzB 54/1 which used a shorter launch tube – 53in compared to the 65in length of the original – making it easier to use under typical field conditions. An even shorter version, the RPzB 54/2, was developed late in 1944, 43in long and weighing 16.5lb, but this does not appear to have reached the production stage. The RPzB 54/1 was approved for service use on December 20, 1944 and at least 25,774 were manufactured from the end of 1944 through war's end, along with about 240,000 of the new short-burn rockets.

OPPOSITE

The Panzerfaust 30 (gross) had an enlarged warhead, based on the type on the HH.3 magnetic antitank grenade. This example is being aimed by a Finnish Army infantryman during the summer 1944 fighting in Finland. (SA-kuva)

THE *PANZERFAUST*

The *Panzerfaust* originated from the same HWA requirement issued to the German ordnance industry in April 1942 for more suitable infantry antitank weapons. Dr. Heinrich Langweiler of HASAG in Leipzig proposed a *Faustpatrone* (Fist projectile), so called because the weapon would be held in one hand prior to launch. The Faustpatrone 43 (FP 43), internally designated as FP 8001, was a small munition, 35cm (13.8in) long with a warhead diameter of 80mm. The projectile weighed about 2.2lb and was ejected from the launch tube using a small black powder propellant charge. The FP 43 was recoilless, ejecting a portion of its exhaust gas out the rear of the launch tube to counteract the front blast. The projectile itself was unpowered.

Trials of the original *Faustpatrone* in the summer of 1942 proved unsatisfactory. The weapon was held by the user at arm's length, which made it nearly impossible to aim the projectile with any accuracy. To exacerbate the accuracy problems further, the projectile proved to be unstable in flight. It relied on spin for stability, but the spin had to be limited, otherwise it would interfere with the shaped-charge effect. Even when the projectile did impact the target, the impact fuze proved to be erratic, dependent on the precise angle of impact, and often failing to detonate at steeper angles. A second version of the projectile was developed with a substantially larger propellant charge, and pop-out fins on the tail section for stability instead of rotation. The launch tube was lengthened and the overall length of the weapon was doubled to 70cm (27.6in) and the weight increased to 5.5lb. In October 1942, HWA clarified the operational requirement, insisting that the weapon have an effective range of at least 30–40m (33–44yd).

By this stage, Langweiler had realized that launching the projectile from arm's length was impractical. By extending the length of the launch tube sufficiently, however, the propellant charge would be burned out before the projectile exited the tube and so the weapon could be fired from the shoulder or from under the arm. Langweiler decided to concentrate on an under-arm launch posture since the small 2oz propellant charge would not provide enough thrust for a flat, horizontal flight, though it did provide enough thrust if angled upward to provide a slow ballistic arc. A simple sight could be added to the launch tube to provide the operator with aiming cues. This third configuration, unveiled in November 1942, proved reasonably successful and could penetrate about 140mm of armor with a maximum range of 30m (33yd).

Another, more powerful version of the *Faustpatrone* was also developed, based on the shaped-charge warhead from the HH.3 magnetic antitank grenade. Owing to the heavier weight of this warhead, the more powerful *Faustpatrone* required nearly double the black powder propellant charge, about 3.4oz. The warhead could penetrate 200mm of armor and had an effective range of 30m (33yd).

The initial version of the *Faustpatrone* with the smaller warhead was designated as FP 1 and the larger as FP 2. Samples of both types

The initial Panzerfaust 30 (klein) had a distinctive, fluted warhead cover as can be seen on this example in the hands of a Luftwaffe soldier in early 1944.

were demonstrated to the HWA at the Kummersdorf proving ground in March 1943 alongside captured American 2.36in bazookas brought back from Tunisia. The trials were intended to determine whether WASAG's 8.8cm RPzB 54 or HASAG's *Faustpatrone* was the preferred choice for the infantry's new antitank weapon. These weapons represented fundamentally different approaches because the 8.8cm RPzB 54 was a crew-served weapon while the *Faustpatrone* was a disposable munition.

In the event, the demand for a potent antitank weapon was so great that the HWA decided to pursue both options. The 8.8cm RPzB 54, renamed *Panzerschreck* for operational use, offered substantially better range and accuracy, albeit at a higher cost; the *Faustpatrone* had superior antiarmor penetration due to its larger warhead, but its accuracy was poor and it could only be launched at close range. The 8.8cm RPzB 54 cost about 70 Reichsmarks per weapon, roughly the same as an MP 40 machine pistol. The typical set of one launcher and ten rockets cost 100 Reichsmarks. The *Faustpatrone* cost about 15–25 Reichsmarks per weapon.

The operational deployment of these weapons was fundamentally different. The *Panzerschreck* was issued to infantry regiments in place of the old antitank rifles, usually 36 per regiment. The *Faustpatrone* was issued as a disposable munition to select riflemen like a hand grenade, so there could be several hundred deployed at any given time in an infantry regiment. Correspondingly, the production requirements were fundamentally different with only about 315,000 *Panzerschreck* launchers and 2.2 million rockets being manufactured compared to over 9 million *Faustpatronen*.

The *Faustpatrone* entered production in August 1943. As in the case of the 8.8cm RPzB 54, the *Faustpatrone* received a new and more belligerent name from Hitler in November 1943: *Panzerfaust* (Armor fist). This name alluded to the Iron Fist of Götz von Berlichingen from the popular 1773 Goethe play. As a result, the FP 1 was usually renamed as *Panzerfaust (klein)* and the FP 2 became *Panzerfaust (gross)*. The term *Faustpatrone* remained the official designation within the German arms industry and Wehrmacht bureaucracy, while the term *Panzerfaust* became the popular name among the troops. There were a variety of other names and abbreviations used for these weapons in official documents, such as F.P. klein 30, F.P. 30, etc. Production of the FP 1/*Panzerfaust (klein)* ended in April 1944, shifting to more powerful versions with larger warheads.

The main shortcoming of the *Panzerfaust* was its short range of 30m (33yd), so the next evolutionary step was to double the range. This was done by increasing the black powder propellant charge to 4.9oz, along with increasing the thickness of the launch tube to accommodate the more powerful launch detonation.

There were a variety of other complaints about the *Panzerfaust* during its early combat use. The trigger assembly was inordinately complicated to manufacture for a disposable weapon. In addition, there were reports from the field about the leakage of exhaust gases from the port where the striker impacted the percussion cap; this resulted in burns to the user's hands or face. The method of arming the weapon proved too complicated in the heat of battle. The threading on the screw joint between the warhead and the projectile body was prone to stripping when the user tried to screw the warhead back in place after arming it with the booster charge and

Panzerfaust launcher technical data

	Panzerfaust 30 (klein)	Panzerfaust 30 (gross)	Panzerfaust 60	Panzerfaust 100
Weight	7.1lb	11.2lb	13.4lb	15.0lb
Projectile weight	3.2lb	6.7lb	6.7lb	6.7lb
Warhead weight	1.8lb	3.5lb	3.5lb	3.5lb
Propellant	1.9oz	3.4oz	4.7oz	6.7oz
Overall length	39in	41in	41in	45in
Warhead diameter	95mm	150mm	150mm	150mm
Launch tube diameter	33mm	44mm	50mm	50mm
Effective range	30m (33yd)	30m (33yd)	60m (66yd)	100m (109yd)
Initial velocity	92ft/sec	98ft/sec	157ft/sec	203ft/sec
Penetration	140mm	200mm	200mm	200mm

fuze. There was also a high dud rate with the warheads because the booster charge tended to fail if it got damp under normal field conditions.

As a result, HASAG redesigned the entire trigger mechanism on the top of the launch tube. The new trigger assembly used simpler, stamped-metal parts and the arming method was made easier. The trigger assembly covered over the percussion cap port to protect the user. The sight was also modified with three apertures to provide the user with different range options of 30m (33yd), 60m (66yd), and 80m (87yd) with the new extended-range version. When this improved version entered production in 1944, the Panzerfaust (gross) was re-designated as Panzerfaust 30, reflecting its range, and the new version was designated as Panzerfaust 60.

Further evolution continued in 1944 with the Panzerfaust 100. There was some reluctance to increase the launch charge, since this would have required a more substantial launch tube, requiring a heavier launcher and a re-tooling of the arms factories producing expensive seamless launch tubes. Instead, HASAG found that two separate launch charges, detonated in sequence with a 2-millisecond interval, provided sufficient impulse to throw the projectile to 150m (164yd) without rupturing the launch tube. The Panzerfaust 100 also introduced a new impact fuze, the FPZ 8003, which was less susceptible to accidental detonation during transport and handling. Development of the Panzerfaust 100 concluded in September 1944 and production began in November 1944. Testing and early combat use revealed accuracy problems that were unexpectedly induced by the greater velocity of the projectile. When the projectile's tail fins were trimmed back from a rectangular to a delta shape, however, the accuracy returned to acceptable standards.

The last version of the Panzerfaust to enter production was the Panzerfaust 150, which entered development in October 1944 with an aim to put it into production in January–February 1945. Unlike the Panzerfaust 100, this was a thorough redesign

PANZERFAUST LAUNCHER EVOLUTION

This illustration shows the first (**1**) and second (**2**) versions of the FP 43, along with the Panzerfaust 30 (klein) (**3**), Panzerfaust 30 (gross) (**4**), Panzerfaust 60 (**5**), Panzerfaust 100 (**6**), Panzerfaust 150 (**7**), and Panzerfaust 250 (**8**).

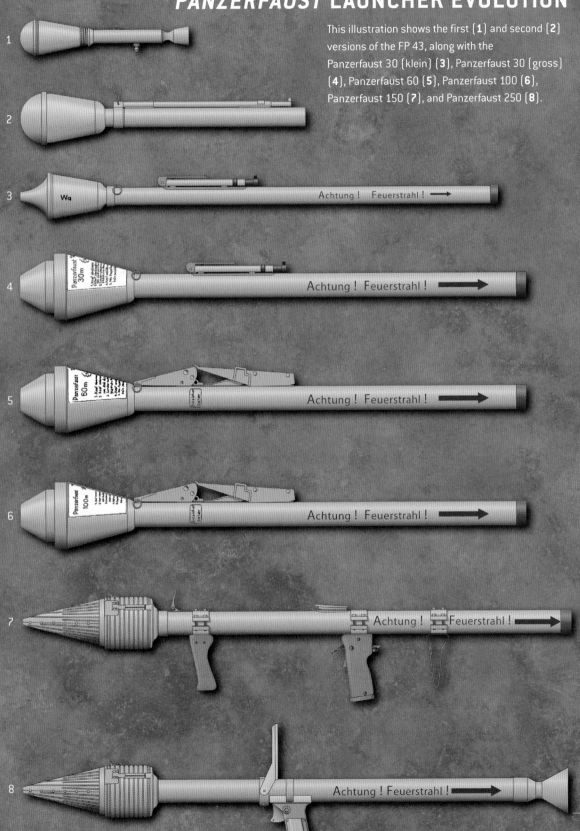

of the weapon. To begin with, the launch tube was no longer disposable, but rather was intended to be re-used. This was due to the growing shortage of the required production materials in Germany at the time. The situation became so desperate that in March 1945, a bonus of three cigarettes was offered for any Panzerfaust 60 or Panzerfaust 100 launch tube returned to the German Army.

The projectile for the Panzerfaust 150 was substantially redesigned with an entirely new nose cone for better penetration. By late 1944, HASAG had recognized that the degree of armor penetration by the warhead could be increased if the warhead detonated at a greater distance from the armor. The increased standoff distance between the impact point and the warhead detonation allowed the high-velocity jet to form a more coherent stream of metal particles. There is some controversy over the penetration capabilities of this warhead. Some accounts claim a penetration increase to 340mm, while postwar Allied interrogations of HASAG officials indicate that it had about the same degree of penetration as the Panzerfaust 100, about 200mm, but that it required much less high explosive to do so.

One of the more curious aspects of the Panzerfaust 150 was the requirement to provide a dual-role capability for use against low-flying aircraft. As a result of this requirement, the warhead could be fitted with a pre-fragmented sleeve around the shaped charge. While this change was simple enough, there was some concern that a large proportion of the projectiles would never hit the targeted aircraft, and were likely to fall to earth creating a menace to troops and civilians. As a result, the FPZ 8003 impact fuze was redesigned as the FPZ 8003 umg (*umgeändert*: modified) with a pyrotechnic timer so that the warhead automatically detonated after about 300m (328yd) of flight, or roughly 2 seconds. This fuze was sometimes issued with late-production Panzerfaust 100 weapons.

The launch method of the Panzerfaust 150 was the same as that of the Panzerfaust 100, using a split, two-part black powder charge. The superior aerodynamics of the projectile provided an effective range of 200m (219yd). The launcher was made of thicker steel in order to be more durable. An initial order for 100,000 Panzerfaust 150 was issued in the spring of 1945 to the Robert Tummler factory in Döbeln, Saxony. Although small-scale production of the Panzerfaust 150 began in March 1945, it is unclear how many, if any, reached troops in the concluding weeks of the war. Indeed, precise details of the series-production launcher are still lacking.

HASAG was in the process of developing the Panzerfaust 250 at the end of the war. This was a further evolution of the Panzerfaust 150, but with a modified launch tube containing a venturi at the end to increase the impulse behind the projectile during launch. Test examples of this weapon had been completed by the end of the war, but serial production was not scheduled to begin until August 1945.

Manufacture of the *Panzerfaust* increased from the initial order for 40,000 per month in October 1943 to 250,000 in August 1944. On September 16, 1944, Hitler ordered a special program to increase production to 1 million per month by November 1944 as a matter of "absolute priority over all others." Production first exceeded 1 million per month in November 1944 and orders increased to 1,500,000 per month from February 1945 to the end of the war in Europe in May. A total of at least

THE EVOLUTION OF *PANZERFAUST* MUNITIONS

This illustration shows the warheads for the Panzerfaust 30 (klein) (**1**), Panzerfaust 30 (gross) (**2**), Panzerfaust 60 (**3**), Panzerfaust 100 (**4**), and Panzerfaust 150 (**5**).

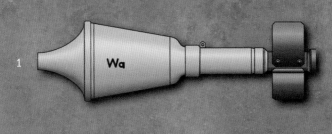

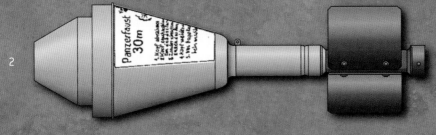

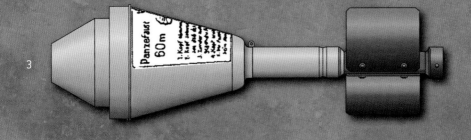

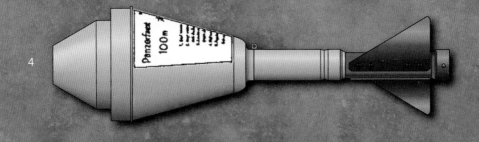

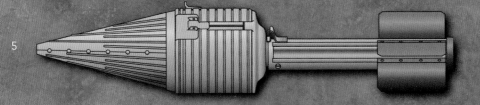

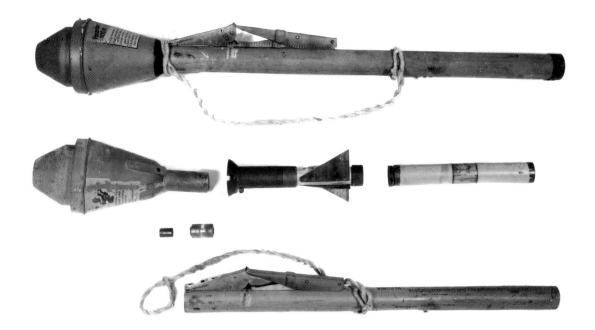

The Panzerfaust 100, depicted here, was very similar in appearance to the earlier Panzerfaust 60. Late-production examples like this one had clipped, delta-shaped fins on the tail section of the warhead instead of the rectangular fins seen on earlier versions.

11,030,000 *Panzerfaust* rounds were ordered during the war. About 4,570,000 rounds were manufactured through the end of 1944 and a further 4,640,000 in 1945 for a total of about 9,210,000. Of these, 2,077,000 were the earlier Panzerfaust 30 (klein) and Panzerfaust 30 (gross) types and the remainder were the later Panzerfaust 60 and Panzerfaust 100.

THE US ARMY ATTEMPTS TO COUNTER SHAPED-CHARGE WEAPONS

Although the US Army had been the first to deploy substantial numbers of antitank rockets in the form of the 2.36in bazooka, there were few efforts made to develop the technical means necessary to protect against antitank weapons. The menace of German *Panzerfaust* and *Panzerschreck* weapons first became evident in the bocage (the French term for farm fields edged in dense hedgerows) fighting in France during June–July 1944 and led to improvised means to protect against shaped-charge warheads.

The US Army separate tank battalions attached to infantry divisions saw the majority of the tank fighting in Normandy in June–July 1944. These tank battalions were managed by Armored Group headquarters and often served as the focus for field improvisations, such as the attempts to develop methods to protect against *Panzerfaust* attack.

The US Army armored divisions were intended for the exploitation mission, and so they were generally held back from large-scale employment until the Operation *Cobra* breakthrough in late July 1944. There were a few exceptions, such as the use of

Combat Command A (CCA), 3d Armored Division at Villiers-Fossard on June 29–30, 1944, but these exceptions only served to confirm the wisdom of refraining from the use of armored divisions in the bocage fighting.

FUSA SANDBAG ARMOR

After encountering increasing numbers of *Panzerschreck* and *Panzerfaust* weapons during the bocage fighting in late June and early July 1944, a number of First US Army (FUSA) tank units began to place improvised sandbag armor on their tanks. This began in the third week of July when the units were in bivouac in preparation for the Operation *Cobra* offensive that started on July 25. There are no known accounts of who came up with the idea of using sandbags – a common field expedient in the US Army for creating defensive strongpoints – as a means of defense against the German antitank weapons. The addition of the sandbags to FUSA tanks took place at the same time that the FUSA Armored Section was overseeing the attachment of "Rhino" hedgerow cutters to the front of tanks, and the application of various forms of tank camouflage in preparation for the offensive.

While it might seem that sandbag armor could be readily fitted to tanks, in fact it required substantial technical support from units other than the tank battalions themselves. The tank battalions did not have stocks of sandbags on hand and had to turn to other units such as engineer battalions to obtain them. Equipping an entire battalion of more than 50 tanks with sandbags required several tons of sand that was not readily on hand. Eventually, trucks had to be sent back to Omaha Beach to collect sufficient sand.

The 32d Armored Regiment, 3d Armored Division fitted sandbags to the glacis plates of its tanks in the days before the start of Operation *Cobra*. This regiment had suffered significant losses to *Panzerfaust* weapons during the fighting for Villiers-Fossard on June 29–30; this is covered in more detail below. Of the 3d Armored Division's two armored regiments, only the 32d showed a special interest in this modification.

The 743d Tank Battalion was the first separate tank battalion to begin systematic application of sandbags to its tanks. This unit had landed on Omaha Beach on D-Day and was in continual combat in the weeks afterward. During July, it supported the 30th Infantry Division in the bocage fighting near Saint-Lô, and was involved in repelling the Panzer-Lehr-Division attack near Le Désert in mid-July. The battalion had encountered German antitank rocket launchers on numerous occasions in June and July 1944. As a result, when the 743d Tank Battalion was sent into bivouac on July 18 in preparation for the forthcoming Operation *Cobra* offensive, a decision was made to fit its tanks with sandbags in the hopes of reducing their vulnerability to the German antitank rocket launchers.

Although the placement of sandbags on the steeply angled front glacis plate presented few problems, side protection proved more difficult. The 743d Tank Battalion still had a few M4A1 DD (Duplex Drive) amphibious tanks from the Omaha Beach landings. These tanks had their canvas skirts removed to enable a narrow metal shelf around the sides to be used for the placing of sandbags. The battalion also began to experiment with welding steel rods to the tank sides to hold additional sandbags. One of the battalion officers suggested the use of jerrycans

Tankers of the 32d Armored Regiment, 3d Armored Division began adding expedient sandbag armor onto their tanks in the wake of the regiment's deadly encounters with *Panzerfaüste* during the fighting for Villiers-Fossard on June 29–30, 1944. This process took place in the days before the start of the Operation *Cobra* offensive on July 25, along with other upgrades such as this attachment of a "Richardson Device" hedgerow cutter (a variation of the "Rhino" hedgerow cutter), shown here in front of an M4A1 (76mm).

attached to the hull sides and filled with sand. Jerrycans were in short supply, however, so only a few of the battalion's tanks received this type of side protection.

The 743d Tank Battalion was under the supervision of the 7th Armored Group, part of VII Corps, FUSA. The battalion's sandbag efforts attracted the attention of the neighboring 3d Armored Group, attached to V Corps, FUSA. There was some controversy over whether the effort was worthwhile, and so V Corps authorized the staff to secure a captured *Panzerschreck* and test fire it against a derelict M4 medium tank fitted with sandbags to see the results. V Corps also wanted to test the sandbags' effectiveness against German rifle grenades. This was due to a lack of understanding of the type of German munitions that had been used against American tanks in the recent fighting. The US Army used an antitank rifle grenade, and so was familiar with this type of weapon, but they had no weapon similar to the *Panzerfaust*. When US troops first saw *Panzerfaust* rocket projectiles descending on tanks, they assumed that they were some form of German rifle grenade.

On the afternoon of July 25, officers from the 741st, 744th, and 759th Tank battalions, as well as from the 3d Armored Group and V Corps headquarters, attended the test firing of the German weapons against a derelict M4 medium tank. Details of this test do not appear to have survived, but the growing threat of German rocket projectiles became very evident in the first few days of Operation *Cobra*. During July 24–27, the 741st Tank Battalion lost at least eight tanks to *Panzerschreck* and *Panzerfaust* strikes. The M5A1 light tanks proved to be especially vulnerable due to their thin armor. On July 27, the 759th Tank Battalion requested 3d Armored Group to obtain steel rods to facilitate the attachment of sandbags to its M5A1 light tanks.

The protection of the thinner side armor of the M5A1 light tank and M4 medium tank remained a technical challenge because there was no simple way to attach sandbags. Another firing test was conducted on July 28 with spaced armor and jerrycans filled with sand. Unit records do not describe what type of spaced armor was used, but this may in fact have been a reference to the jerrycans themselves rather than an additional layer of steel armor. The test found that the improvised jerrycan armor was effective against rifle grenades but that it did not diminish the degree of penetration by the *Panzerschreck* rocket projectile. Following the test, the reports were forwarded to the FUSA Armored Section which was starting to show interest in this idea due to the number of losses to *Panzerschreck* strikes during Operation *Cobra*.

The increasing number of US Army encounters with *Panzerfaust* and *Panzerschreck* projectiles in the summer fighting led to greater attention to these threats by higher headquarters. In August 1944, the Armored Section of Maj. Gen. Omar N. Bradley's 12th Army Group headquarters dispatched teams to interview tank units in Normandy to learn any lessons from the recent fighting. One of the Armored Section teams visited the 11th Armored Group in mid-August 1944 which managed the 712th, 735th, and 749th Tank battalions. The subsequent report from this team noted that "the majority of tank losses have been from enemy bazooka fire." The general consensus among the tank battalion commanders was that "The only defense known is close support from the infantry." The tank battalions had quickly learned that close cooperation with the infantry kept the German antitank rocket teams far enough away from the American tanks that they were considerably less dangerous.

TECHNICAL ALTERNATIVES

On August 8, 1944, the European Theater of Operations-US Army (ETOUSA) headquarters sent a request back to Ordnance in the United States to inquire whether they had any new technologies to defeat shaped-charge warheads, especially the infantry rocket weapons. In fact, Ordnance had begun such a program in October 1943. There were two principal approaches: plastic armor and spikes.

In October 1943, Ordnance awarded a contract to the Flintkote Company to develop "plastic armor" to protect tanks against shaped-charge warheads. Plastic armor had been developed in 1940 by Edward Terrell of the British Admiralty as a less expensive means to protect British merchant ships than conventional steel armor. It usually consisted of a mixture of asphalt, concrete or some other form of aggregate. Flintkote developed a type of plastic armor that consisted of quartz gravel in a matrix of asphalt and wood flour (sawdust). The objective of the program was to provide 80 percent protection against Panzerfaust 30 (gross) and 100 percent protection against Panzerfaust 30 (klein) warheads. The armor had to be durable enough to withstand the impact of 105mm field artillery and to provide the equivalent of an additional 2in (51mm) of steel armor against German 7.5cm antitank guns.

The Flintkote Company's HCR2 plastic armor system was developed in 1943–45 to protect the M4 medium tank from penetration by shaped-charge weapons such as the *Panzerfaust*. Although technically successful, there was never enough priority assigned to the program to push it into production in time for combat use in the European Theater of Operations.

Flintkote eventually developed the HCR2 plastic armor that consisted of modular panels with a 10in (254mm)-thick layer of the quartz matrix faced with 1in (25mm) aluminum plate. This was capable of defeating the newer Panzerfaust 100 and the *Panzerschreck* warhead. Owing to a lack of priority on the program, however, the engineering effort to develop a convenient method of mounting the plastic armor was not completed until the summer of 1945. The HCR2 system added 3 tons of weight to the M4's turret and 4 tons to the hull, as well as widening the hull by 21in due to the thickness of the hull modules. Although the HCR2 plastic armor did offer sufficient protection against the *Panzerfaust* threat, there was never enough urgency to rush the kit into production and development was not concluded until September 1945.

Besides the field army modification programs, some US Army units developed their own unique expedient armor. This is an M4A3E8 of the 18th Tank Battalion, 8th Armored Division in Bocholtz, Netherlands, north of Aachen, on February 23, 1945. Besides the usual sandbags on the glacis plate, it had track links welded to the turret sides and captured jerrycans filled with sand attached to the hull side.

This M4 of the 747th Tank Battalion in Schleiden, Germany, on January 31, 1945 reveals the basic layer of welded track links that formed the basis of NUSA's expedient armor system, but the sandbags and camouflage net have not yet been fitted.

The second technical approach to the *Panzerfaust* threat was to fit spikes to the armor. These were 1in-diameter steel rods, 7–8in high, spaced about 2.5in apart. When a shaped-charge warhead struck a spike, the impact deformed the warhead sufficiently to prevent the proper formation of the penetrating jet of metal particles. Studies concluded that the fitting of spikes would add 4.1 tons to the weight of an M4 medium tank. In the event, fabrication of this system for tanks proved to be too great a challenge. Small-scale test examples of spike armor were fabricated and tested, but no tank was actually fully fitted with this system during the war.

FURTHER IMPROVISATIONS

Although the *Panzerfaust* and *Panzerschreck* were encountered in increasing numbers during the fighting in the fall of 1944, the US Army assigned little urgency to the *Panzerfaust* and *Panzerschreck* threat until November 1944, by which time the FUSA tank

A pair of M4A3 (76mm) tanks of the 747th Tank Battalion in Schleiden, Germany, on January 31, 1945 after the addition of the NUSA expedient armor had been completed. The basic layer of track links was followed by a layer of sandbags and camouflage netting.

The appearance of mesh aprons on the PzKpfw IV Ausf J in late 1944 led the US Army to the mistaken belief it was intended for anti-bazooka protection. Tests by the 1st Armored Group in Alsace in January 1945 using *Panzerschreck* launchers against improvised screens demonstrated that it had no protective value.

reports showed an increasing proportion of casualties caused by *Panzerfaust* and *Panzerschreck* strikes during the fall of 1944. Starting at only about 4 percent of the identified tank casualties in September, the casualty rate rose to 12.5 percent in October and 14.6 percent in November. The increase in casualties during November 1944 largely stemmed from the Operation *Queen* offensive along the Roer River where larger numbers of German rocket weapons were encountered, and where the built-up, industrialized towns in the area favored the use of close-attack weapons. Anticipating these problems, the 2d Armored Division had begun adding sandbags to the front of its tanks in preparation for the Operation *Queen* offensive.

Another improvisation widely seen on US Army tanks operating in the ETO at this time was the attachment of log mats. This usually consisted of three or more logs, wired together and carried either on the hull side or bow of the tank. At first glance, this might seem to be improvised protection. In fact, it was a method used to help the tank traverse the thick mud that was an increasing nuisance during the unusually wet fall of 1944.

In December 1944–January 1945, in the wake of Operation *Queen*, the Ninth US Army (NUSA) led another round of improvised armor application in preparation for the forthcoming Operation *Grenade* advance to the Rhine River. The NUSA expedient armor was more elaborate than the simple sandbag armor that had been applied by FUSA in July 1944. It was layered and consisted of an initial layer of steel track links welded to the hull, followed by a layer of sandbags, and finally a covering of camouflage net to help keep the sandbags in place. This system was applied to a number of the separate tank battalions in NUSA as well as many tanks of the 2d Armored Division. This was one of the only US expedient armor sets that used track links, probably due to the fact that NUSA was the northernmost of the US field

The SUSA expedient armor package began with the addition of steel cages to the hull and turret of its tanks to hold the sandbags. This is a new M4A3E8 of the 191st Tank Battalion in Graufthal, Alsace, on March 1, 1945, with the cage being welded to the turret.

armies and adjacent to the British/Canadian 21st Army Group. The British and Canadians had made extensive use of steel track blocks as supplementary armor since the summer of 1944, largely as an antidote to the threat posed by German antitank guns rather than the *Panzerfaust*.

The most extensive application of expedient armor on US Army tanks operating in the ETO took place in February–March 1945 in the wake of the German winter offensives. This mainly involved two separate efforts by Lt. Gen. George S. Patton's Third US Army (TUSA) and Lt. Gen. Alexander M. Patch's Seventh US Army (SUSA). Patton had been convinced by his Ordnance officers that sandbags were ineffective and a potential handicap to tank performance due to their weight. However, tank fighting in the Ardennes had led to widespread complaints about the poor armor protection of the M4 medium tank. In lieu of sandbag armor, the Ordnance Section of TUSA recommended the

With the steel cages fitted to the tank, the crew could then fill the frames with sandbags as shown here at Graufthal on March 1, 1945.

use of armor plate stripped off derelict American and German tanks. This was not specifically aimed at countering the *Panzerfaust*, but rather as a general upgrade to the tank armor versus all antitank threats.

The 326th Ordnance Maintenance Battalion in Esch, Luxembourg, was assigned the task of cannibalizing wrecked tanks for their armor.

SUSA's 12th Armored Division was not entirely convinced about sandbag armor and experimented with reinforced-concrete armor as an alternative. This is an example of an M4A3E8 fitted with more than 1ft (305mm) of concrete on the glacis plate, and 7–9in (178–229mm) on the hull side.

The process of attaching the armor to tanks took about 85 man-hours per tank, and eventually TUSA contracted three Belgian factories to undertake the work. Priority was given to the 4th, 6th, and 11th Armored divisions, the three armored divisions subordinate to TUSA. Each armored division was issued 36 up-armored tanks, with additional tanks following as and when time and resources permitted.

SUSA in Alsace had suffered significant tank losses in January 1945, and agreed to permit Patton's salvage crews to cannibalize its tanks as well. The reason that SUSA permitted the cannibalization of tank armor by TUSA was that SUSA had its own armor upgrade program. The main concern in SUSA was the *Panzerfaust* and *Panzerschreck* threat due to heavy losses suffered by the 12th Armored Division during the fighting around Herrlisheim and losses of the 14th Armored Division around Rittershofen during the German Operation *Nordwind* offensive of December 31, 1944 to January 25, 1945.

Patton's TUSA banned sandbag armor and preferred to weld additional armor plate to its tanks. This is an M4A3E8 of the 11th Armored Division with armor plate added to the turret and hull front.

M4A3E8 WITH SUSA EXPEDIENT ARMOR

25th TANK BATTALION, 14th ARMORED DIVISION, APRIL 1945, GERMANY

Crew: 5 (commander, gunner, loader, driver, co-driver)

Combat weight: 37.1 tons combat loaded + 3 tons of sandbags

Power-to-weight ratio: 12.5hp/T

Overall length: 24.2ft

Width: 9.8ft

Height: 11.2ft

Engine: Ford GAA 8 cylinder, 500hp at 2,600rpm

Transmission: Syncromesh with 5 forward, 1 reverse speed with two-plate dry disc clutch

Fuel capacity: 172 gallons

Maximum speed (road): 24mph

Maximum speed (cross-country): 16mph

Range: 100 miles

Fuel consumption: 1.7 gallons per mile

Ground pressure: 11.0psi

Main armament: 76mm M1A1 gun in M62 combination mount with .30-cal. coaxial machine gun

Secondary armament: .50-cal. Browning M2 HB HMG on turret; .30-cal. Browning LMG in hull

Main gun ammunition: 71 rounds 76mm

Armor: 89mm (gun mantlet); 63mm (turret side); 63–108mm (hull front); 38mm (hull side)

24.2ft

11.2ft

9.8ft

TUSA cannibalized armor from knocked-out American and German tanks for its expedient armor program. This is an M4(105mm) assault gun that has lost its glacis plate and side hull armor to Patton's scavengers.

The 1st Armored Group headquarters was serving as the armored section for VI Corps, SUSA. As early as January 2, 1945, this headquarters had been testing methods to defeat shaped-charge warheads. SUSA had encountered PzKpfw IV Ausf. J medium tanks fitted with *Schürzen* (mesh aprons) and there was widespread belief that these "bazooka skirts" were intended to defeat American shaped-charge warheads such as those fired from the 2.36in bazooka. In fact, they were a variation on the existing steel-plate aprons and were intended to defeat Soviet 14.5mm antitank rifles. In the event, the 1st Armored Group cobbled together its own versions of the mesh skirts, fitted them to a captured PzKpfw IV tank, and fired at them with a captured *Panzerschreck*. The test showed conclusively that the mesh skirts were completely ineffective against shaped-charge warheads.

The SUSA AFV Section was convinced that a systematic application of sandbags was the solution to the shaped-charge threat. In contrast to earlier sandbag schemes, however, SUSA came up with a modification package that began by welding steel cages to the hull and turret of its M4 medium tanks to contain the sandbags. This modification package also involved a much thicker layer of sandbags, generally two sandbags thick on the hull and turret sides and two to four sandbags thick on the glacis plate. The addition of steel cages and sandbags added about 3 tons to the weight of the tank.

This elaborate effort was overseen by Ordnance units, but much of the actual work was carried out by divisional maintenance battalions. In February–March 1945, this program refitted virtually all of the tanks of the 12th and 14th Armored divisions, as well as those of the separate tank battalions under the 1st Armored Group.

One of the main problems with the SUSA sandbag modification package was that the sandbags on the front hull still were prone to fall off when jostled during movement. As a result, the 23d Tank Battalion, 12th Armored Division began experimenting with concrete armor on the glacis plate. The standard configuration was created by welding .75in bolts to the glacis plate at 12in intervals. Two layers of heavy wire mesh were then welded to the bolts. The first layer was 2in (51mm) from the surface and the second was 4in (102mm) from the surface. Finally, steel rebar reinforcing rods were welded to the ends of the bolts. Wooden forms were then attached and the concrete poured.

The 709th Tank Battalion, subordinate to 1st Armored Group in SUSA, also began experimenting with poured concrete armor on its tanks in March 1945. Tests were conducted using the Panzerfaust 60 against derelict tanks fitted with the expedient concrete armor. The battalion operations officer, Maj. John Cochran, noted that the *Panzerfaust* "could penetrate both armor plates and concrete, but the splash of the shell inside the tank was negligible." In other words, the concrete absorbed so much of the energy of the penetrating jet, that by the time it bore through the armor plate, most of its energy was spent. Reinforced concrete was more successful than sandbags because it was denser.

By March 1945, a significant proportion of US Army tanks operating in the ETO had received some form of expedient armor. All four of the US field armies had developed some type of expedient armor in 1944–45, though these packages were not universally applied to their tanks. The Fifteenth US Army, which deployed to the Ruhr sector only in April 1945, saw little combat, and did not develop its own expedient armor.

Seven of the 15 armored divisions in the ETO (2d, 3d, 4th, 6th, 11th, 12th, and 14th) were equipped with tanks fitted with expedient armor by 1945. The separate tank battalions in the ETO present a much more mixed picture of coverage since these smaller units often did not have the resources to apply expedient armor in any systematic fashion. Some separate tank battalions, such as those with SUSA in Alsace, tended to have more thorough coverage due to a more vigorous promotion of the effort by senior commanders. In other armies, coverage depended on time,

After the 3d Armored Division took part in the capture of Cologne on March 6, 1945, the unit took advantage of stockpiles of steel plate in nearby factories to add additional armor to the front of its tanks. This is an M4A1 (76mm) of the 3d Armored Division near Korbach, Germany, on March 30, 1945, with a double layer of steel attached to the hull front.

In the final months of war, several units began to experiment with reinforced concrete as an alternative to sandbags. Pictured on March 19, 1945, in Gelsenkirchen, Germany, this M4A3(76mm) of the 2d Armored Division has improvised reinforced-concrete armor on the glacis plate.

circumstance, and the availability of resources. For example, the 3d Armored Division managed to fit additional steel armor on many of its tanks after the capture of Cologne in March 1945, where a local factory provided a source of steel plate and welding equipment.

DEVELOPMENTS IN OTHER ARMIES

It is worth noting that the controversy over the value of sandbag armor extended to the armed forces of other countries, including the Wehrmacht. In December 1944, the Waffenschule (weapons school) of 4. Panzerarmee on the Eastern Front reported that wire-mesh aprons as well as *elastiche Schürzen* ("resilient aprons") could degrade the effectiveness of *Panzerfaust* and *Panzerschreck* impacts. The Red Army had captured large quantities of *Panzerfäuste* and were using them against German tanks. As a result, the HWA instructed HASAG in Leipzig to test the *Panzerfaust* against plate and mesh aprons as well as various types of fabric aprons made from burlap that had been promoted by 4. Panzerarmee's Waffenschule as a solution to the shaped-charge threat. HASAG reported that tests on December 3, 1944 had shown that the aprons did not degrade the penetration of shaped-charge warheads. These tests were followed by similar tests at the Kummersdorf proving ground on December 21, 1944 using actual PzKpfw IV and captured M4 medium tanks fitted with various aprons and sandbags. Once again, the trials showed that the aprons did not diminish the performance of shaped-charge warheads.

British and Canadian tank units made extensive use of steel track blocks as supplementary armor, but this was primarily intended to deal with German tank and antitank guns rather than shaped-charge weapons. Owing to the increasing threat of shaped-charge weapons in February 1945, the First Canadian Army in cooperation with the British Army's Directorate of Tank Design (DTD) began field trials of expedient armor arrays. The different systems tested included spaced steel armor; spaced armor backed by fillers such as cord, rockwool, or sand; steeply angled plates to defeat the *Panzerfaust* impact fuze; spikes to prevent the proper

function of the shaped charge; and soft mesh screens to catch the *Panzerfaust* and thus prevent warhead detonation.

Spaced armor was effective when placed at least 30in (76cm) from the main armor. However, this increased the width of the tank by 5ft, which was not considered practical. A 20mm steel plate placed about 12in (30cm) from the main armor actually enhanced *Panzerfaust* penetration because it optimized the standoff distance and allowed the penetrating jet to form more coherently. Spaced armor filled with 12in (30cm) of sand was effective but the package added 5–9 tons to the tank's weight. Spikes were effective against the Panzerfaust 30 (klein) but not the more common Panzerfaust 60. Soft mesh screens did manage to foil the Panzerfaust 30 (klein) because that weapon had an impact energy of only 440ft/lb, but they were not successful in stopping the Panzerfaust 60, which had an impact energy of about 3,500ft/lb. As a result of these tests, there was no systematic effort to create counter-*Panzerfaust* expedient armor in Field Marshal Bernard L. Montgomery's 21st Army Group.

The Red Army also suffered increasing losses to the *Panzerfaust* in 1945. During the fighting for Berlin, Maj. Gen. Boris A. Anisimov, the armored forces commander of the 5th Shock Army, instructed subordinate units to install special counter-*Panzerfaust* screens on their tanks. These screens were based on available supplies of metal mesh made from 0.5–0.8mm wire with 40×40mm spacing. The mesh was welded to rectangular frames made from 15–20mm steel rod. The frames were then welded to the tank at a distance of 200mm from the tank's armor. While these have sometimes been described as bed-springs "liberated" from German homes, the frames were actually manufactured by field workshops specifically for tank defense. Special attention was paid to mounting the frames on the tank's upper surfaces due to the frequent use of *Panzerfaust* weapons from the upper floors of buildings against the tops of Soviet tanks in the streets below. A postwar Soviet report credited these screens as having been effective in degrading the *Panzerfaust* performance, even though this contradicts the findings of other armies in 1945.

The Red Army also faced the *Panzerfaust* problem. During the battle for Berlin in April–May 1945, the 5th Shock Army added counter-*Panzerfaust* screens to its tanks to deal with the threat, as shown on this T-34-85 medium tank in front of the Brandenburg Gate.

TECHNICAL
SPECIFICATIONS

PANZERFAUST FIRING PROCEDURE

The Panzerfaust 30 had an intricate safeing and arming system to prevent accidental detonation of its large warhead. Prior to use, the impact fuze (*Zünder*)

To arm the *Panzerfaust*, a soldier had to remove the warhead from the body of the munition, take out the package containing the booster charge and impact fuze and place them in proper sequence behind the warhead before reassembling the munition into its launch tube. This is an illustration from the *Panzerfaust* manual.

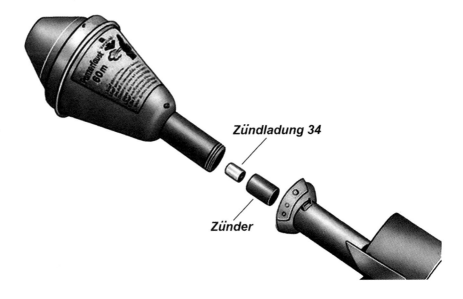

Zündladung 34

Zünder

PANZERFAUST SIGHT

The *Panzerfaust* leaf sight was folded upward as part of the munition-arming sequence. To aim the weapon, the user would first estimate the range to the target. On the sight were three range gates for 30m, 60m, and 80m. The user would then aim through the appropriate range gate, aligning the small "V" notch at the bottom with the small metal pip on the top of the warhead. Once the weapon was aimed, the trigger behind the sight was squeezed downward to activate the propulsion charge.

and booster charge (Zündladung 34) were kept separate from the weapon. To arm the warhead, the soldier unscrewed the warhead from the rest of the rocket projectile, and inserted the booster charge and impact fuze into the cylindrical openings at the base of the warhead. He then screwed the warhead back on to the weapon. As a further safety measure, the rocket projectile could not be launched until after the leaf sight was folded upward. The sight was held in place by a cotter pin which was removed before folding the sight upward. Once this was done, the trigger assembly could be cocked via a spring-loaded bolt in the trigger assembly on top of the rocket projectile, behind the sight. When activated, the bolt popped out a small trigger button on the assembly. To aim the *Panzerfaust*, the user peered through a sight aperture, aligning it with a small marking at the top of the warhead. When the trigger was depressed, the striker bolt moved forward, hitting a small percussion cap within the assembly, and igniting the propellant charge.

At very short ranges, the Panzerfaust 30 could be fired from the shoulder. However, to obtain the maximum range of 30m (33yd), the recommended posture was to place the weapon under the arm, which forced the user to position the weapon at an upward angle. Soldiers were warned about the back-blast when the weapon was detonated. The instructions recommended a distance of at least 10m (11yd) from any wall or other large object.

The *Panzerfaust* proved to be a danger to its users when first introduced, largely due to sloppy handling practices. Once the impact fuze and booster charge were placed into the rear of the warhead, the high explosives could be readily detonated. Some troops began this stage of the arming process in advance to make it easier to use the *Panzerfaust* once enemy tanks appeared. However, if the weapon was accidentally dropped on its head against a hard surface, the impact fuze often proved sensitive enough to detonate the warhead. During one training incident near Paris in the summer of 1944, an instructor accidentally dropped an armed *Panzerfaust* on the ground, detonating the warhead and several nearby and killing some 100 students. These dangers were negated by more vigorous training of troops issued the *Panzerfaust*.

PANZERSCHRECK FIRING PROCEDURE

To fire the *Panzerschreck*, the gunner began by pulling back the safety trigger at the front of the main trigger assembly. This safety feature prevented the main launch trigger from being depressed, and so avoided an accidental rocket launch during the loading process. This also cocked the firing pin into its forward position. Once this was done, the loader could insert the rocket into the rear of the launch tube. The rocket was pushed forward enough to be flush with the rear of the tube, activating a small safety catch at the bottom of the tube that prevented the rocket from sliding back out. In addition, the loader had to be careful to push the rocket in deep enough to engage a spring-loaded contact at the top of the tube that was a principal

A comparison of the standard, mid-production RPzB 54 (below) and the shortened RPzB 54/1 (above).

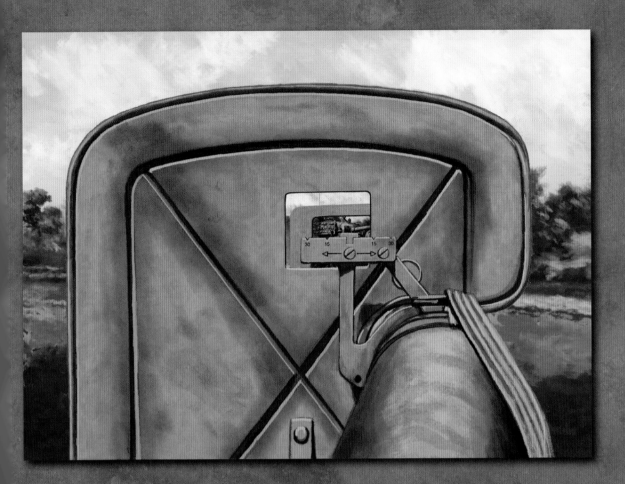

PANZERSCHRECK SIGHTS

The *Panzerschreck* had a pair of sights. The sight at the front of the launch tube had range gates for 100m, 150m, and 200m. The rear sight had a central aiming "V" groove used when firing against stationary targets. There was also a pair of "V" grooves on either side of the main aiming point to provide compensation for moving targets depending on their crossing speed and direction. The user chose the appropriate "V" groove, and then aligned it with the appropriate range gate "pip" before squeezing the firing trigger.

connection in the firing circuit. Dangling from the end of the rocket was a set of wires leading to a small wooden contact block. The loader clipped the block to the firing circuit at the rear top of the launch tube to complete the firing circuit. Once the rocket was loaded, the gunner could then arm the launcher by depressing a small clip within the safety trigger in front of the handgrip, releasing it from the safety position. The gunner would estimate the range to the target, then aim the *Panzerschreck* using the stadia in the forward sight corresponding to the range. When the gunner depressed the launch trigger, it released the firing pin that struck the *Stoßgenerator* (surge generator) behind the handle. This sent an electrical impulse to the rocket, igniting the rocket motor and launching the rocket.

PANZERFAUST EFFECTIVENESS

Wartime shaped-charge weapons offered phenomenal antiarmor penetration compared to tank and antitank guns using conventional kinetic-energy projectiles. For example, the 75mm gun on the M4 medium tank could penetrate about 70mm of armor, angled at 30 degrees, at 500m (547yd). The 8.8cm gun on the Tiger I heavy tank could penetrate about 110mm of steel armor at 30 degrees at 500m (547yd) – about half the penetration of the *Panzerschreck*'s 8.8cm shaped-charge warhead.

This raises an obvious question. If shaped-charge warheads were so powerful, why weren't they used in conjunction with tank guns? There were two technical reasons why World War II tanks did not use shaped-charge warheads. First, tank guns in World War II used rifled barrels to stabilize the projectiles and improve their accuracy by means of rotation. However, rapid rotation substantially degraded the effectiveness of shaped-charge warheads. Second, early shaped-charge warheads used simple impact fuzes to initiate the detonation sequence, whereas tank projectiles were so fast that the warhead liner was usually crushed before it formed its penetrating jet of metal particles. So there were some shaped-charge projectiles in use in World War II, usually fired from howitzers that had a relatively slow velocity, but they were not used in conjunction with most tank guns.

Rocket launchers such as the US bazooka and German *Panzerschreck*, and grenade projectors such as the British PIAT (Projector Infantry Anti-Tank) and German *Panzerfaust*, were very well suited to early shaped-charge warheads. Their projectiles did not have rapid rotation and were slow enough that the penetrating jet had enough time to form following the warhead impact.

The *Panzerfaust* was arguably the most revolutionary of the wartime shaped-charge weapons. It was a disposable munition rather than a crew-served weapon and so was issued in massive numbers by 1945. Not surprisingly, a number of technical assessments of the *Panzerfaust* were conducted by Allied armies. The US Army Ground Forces headquarters was interested in whether a weapon similar to the *Panzerfaust* should be adopted by the US infantry and directed some captured examples to be shipped to the Infantry Board at Fort Benning, Georgia. The Infantry Board wanted a mixture of Panzerfaust 60 and Panzerfaust 100 but in the event, 20 Panzerfaust 100 arrived in April 1946. They were tested alongside 2.36in and 3.5in bazookas for comparative purposes. The Infantry Board concluded that the Panzerfaust 100 offered antiarmor penetration superior to that offered by the 2.36in bazooka, but inferior to that offered by the new 3.5in bazooka. The *Panzerfaust* was more effective than either bazooka against sandbags and concrete. However, the Infantry Board was unhappy with the amount of smoke produced by the *Panzerfaust* on firing, its short range, and the crudity of its design, especially the elementary sights and the long trigger pull. The Infantry Board recommended that the US Army adopt a similar, but improved weapon. In the event, this did not occur due to the sharp decline in US Army budgets in the wake of World War II. It was not until 1963 that the US Army adopted a disposable antitank rocket, the M72 LAW (Light Anti-tank (or Anti-armor) Weapon, that was substantially different in technical features to the *Panzerfaust*.

The Infantry Board tests showed that the Panzerfaust 100 could reliably penetrate 8in (203mm) of armor, but not 10in (254mm). Tests were also conducted against

PANZERFAUST SHAPED-CHARGE IMPACT SEQUENCE

The warhead impact sets off the impact fuze and booster charge (**1**). The main warhead charge is detonated by the impact fuze and booster charge (**2**); the detonation begins to deform the warhead's conical metal liner into a high-velocity particle jet. Once the particle jet is formed, it penetrates through the armor (**3**), spraying the tank interior with a lethal overpressure blast and incandescent spall.

concrete walls and sandbags of the types that might be used for defensive strongpoints, and the results of these tests have some relevance to the use of concrete and sandbags as improvised armor on US Army tanks. A Panzerfaust 100 fired against a reinforced-concrete wall 3ft (91cm) thick – substantially thicker than the concrete added to the tanks – did not penetrate the entire wall, but did cause it to crack. Another Panzerfaust 100 was fired against a sandbag wall that was 4ft (122cm) high and 3ft (91cm) thick. The *Panzerfaust* completely demolished the sandbag wall and caused noticeable damage behind it.

To test the accuracy of the *Panzerfaust*, three of the weapons were placed on a fixed mount and fired at a target 50yd away. Horizontal dispersion was poor, averaging 70in, while vertical dispersion was excellent, only 3in.

The shaped-charge warhead of the *Panzerfaust* creates a very distinctive, circular spall pattern on detonating against armor plate. This is an example of a Panzerfaust 100 detonation.

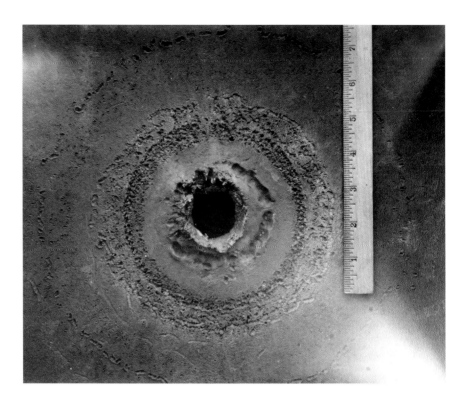

A British operations research study of *Panzerfaust* attacks on British/Canadian tanks east of the Rhine River in 1945 shows, not surprisingly, that the majority of engagements took place at ranges under 60yd, the nominal range of the Panzerfaust 60.

Panzerfaust engagement range					
Range	0–20yd	21–40yd	41–60yd	61–80yd	81–100yd	100yd+
Hits	35	22	13	4	3	3
Misses	15	14	13	5	4	7

It is worth noting that the Wehrmacht conducted a survey of *Panzerfaust* use on the Eastern Front and found that there was 1 tank kill per 2,594 *Panzerfaust* launches. While this might suggest a woeful lack of accuracy, a large proportion of *Panzerfäuste*, perhaps the majority, were used as a general assault weapon against targets other than tanks.

There were a variety of reasons for the *Panzerfaust*'s low kill rate. To begin with, the weapon had to be used at very close ranges and so the user was vulnerable to enemy fire while arming and aiming the weapon. As mentioned before, US Army tests of the Panzerfaust 100 found that the *Panzerfaust* suffered from relatively high lateral dispersion, thus reducing its accuracy. From a technical perspective, the weapon's performance was highly dependent on an accurate range estimate by the user. After estimating the range, the user then used the appropriate aperture on the *Panzerfaust* sight. This was not easy to do in the heat of battle. If the soldier made a poor judgment, the *Panzerfaust* rocket projectile could easily fly over the target tank or fall short.

Even if the *Panzerfaust* struck the target tank, there were a variety of reasons for it to fail to penetrate. The most common problem was the booster charge inserted by the user before firing that detonated the main warhead once activated by the impact fuze. These small charges were susceptible to absorbing moisture in humid conditions, and then failing to detonate. The impact fuze usually had a high success rate if the *Panzerfaust* struck the enemy tank squarely; but if it struck the tank at an oblique angle, the impact fuze would sometimes fail to detonate properly. Another problem occurred if the *Panzerfaust* was fired from too close a range. If it impacted the enemy tank at too great a speed, the shaped-charge liner was crushed or deformed before the penetrating jet had formed properly. As mentioned in the biography of Staff Sergeant Lafayette Pool (see page 59), his M4 medium tank was hit by four *Panzerfaust* projectiles without suffering any damage; but the fifth one knocked out his tank.

FUSA SANDBAG ARMOR EFFECTIVENESS

Was US sandbag armor effective in diminishing the destructive power of German antitank rockets? This remained an enduring controversy through the rest of the campaign in the ETO. Many US Army units felt that sandbags were nearly worthless and that their significant weight reduced the mobility of their tanks and caused suspension damage. Other units felt that sandbags were worthwhile.

The 743d Tank Battalion was one of the pioneers of sandbag armor. Besides placing it on the front of its tanks, the battalion made various attempts to mount it on the sides of the tanks as well. This is an example of an M4A1 (76mm) with a shelf added to the hull sides to permit the addition of a layer of sandbags.

In purely technical terms, sandbags had very limited protective effects. US Army sandbags were typically 14–17in (36–43cm) wide. As shown in the accompanying table, the German shaped-charge warheads could penetrate 50–72in (127–183cm) of sandbags. While sandbags could diminish the degree of penetration achieved by the warhead, usually there was still enough residual energy left in the warhead to penetrate the glacis plate of the M4 medium tank. US Army Ordnance officers felt that shaped-charge warheads needed at least 2in (51mm) of penetrating power beyond the energy needed to penetrate the armor plate in order to cause significant damage within the tank. To be effective against a tank such as the M4 with its 90mm (equivalent) frontal armor required a warhead with 140mm penetrating power (90+50mm) to have lethal internal effects – well within the capability of even the small *Panzerfaust*.

Penetration of the M4 medium tank's frontal armor was highly dependent on the precise angle of impact. Roughly speaking, the M4's steel glacis armor had an effective thickness to frontal attack of about 90mm. The early- and mid-production M4 tanks had 2in (51mm) of armor at 56° (90mm effective thickness), while the later "large hatch" M4 tanks had 2.5in (64mm) of armor at 47° (93mm effective thickness). If the weakest of the German weapons, the Panzerfaust 30 (klein), hit a sandbag-protected M4 tank frontally, less than one-third of its energy would be expended penetrating the sandbag, leaving it with the capability of penetrating an additional 100mm of steel armor. In the case of the Panzerfaust 30 (gross), residual penetration power was over 150mm. In either case, it was enough to penetrate the tank, though the Panzerfaust 30 (klein) had markedly reduced behind-armor effects when enough energy was absorbed by the sandbags.

There was also the issue of standoff. Early shaped-charge warheads depended on simple impact fuzes for detonation, and a certain proportion failed to detonate properly when striking angled surfaces. Sandbags provided a surface better suited to warhead detonation and less susceptible to the effects of ricochet. Furthermore, detonation of the warhead a few inches away from the glacis plate may have enhanced the penetration of the tank's armor since it provided a few milliseconds more for the warhead high-velocity particle jet to form properly.

Comparative warhead penetration				
	Warhead diameter	Rolled homogenous (steel) armor	Sandbags	Reinforced concrete
Panzerfaust 30 (klein)	100mm	140mm	50in (127cm)	10in (25cm)
Panzerfaust 30 (gross), Panzerfaust 60, Panzerfaust 100	150mm	200mm	72in (183cm)	14in (36cm)
Panzerschreck	88mm	160mm	60in (152cm)	12in (30cm)

This does not mean that sandbag protection was worthless, however. At some impact angles, particularly rocket impacts at acute angles from the side against the glacis plate, the warhead would have to penetrate more than one sandbag. In turn, it would also have to penetrate the glacis plate at a steeper angle, giving the tank armor greater effective thickness. In these circumstances, sandbags could provide a sufficient

US ARMY EXPEDIENT ARMOR TYPES

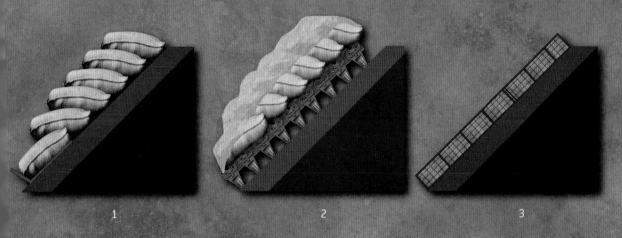

1	2	3

This illustration shows three types of expedient armor types developed by the US Army. The expedient armor (**1**) used by FUSA in the summer of 1944 employed a layer of sandbags. The layered armor (**2**) employed by NUSA from December 1944 through February 1945 featured a layer of sandbags placed over tank tracks and covered with camouflage netting. The concrete armor (**3**) developed by SUSA during February–March 1945 was made using .75in bolts, heavy wire mesh, steel rebar reinforcing rods, and poured concrete.

margin to limit or prevent penetration of the tank armor, or to limit the internal damage once penetration occurred.

The interaction of a shaped-charge warhead and a sandbag/armor target was difficult to predict with any precision due to many variables including the varying thickness of sandbags, and the composition of the sandbag fill. Different types of sand offered different densities and thus different resistance to penetration. Furthermore, wet sand has greater resistance to penetration than dry sand. Besides these variables, the manufacturing quality of the German warheads and impact fuzes had their own irregularities, leading to erratic performance under combat conditions. As a result of these complexities, the effectiveness of sandbag armor under shaped-charge attack was extremely variable. No study was ever undertaken to establish the percentage of times that sandbag armor succeeded or failed, and so the debate over sandbag effectiveness relied entirely on anecdotal evidence and hearsay.

TESTING THE SUSA SANDBAG ARMOR

As in the case of previous sandbag programs, there was some skepticism as to the actual protective value of the SUSA modification package fitted in February–March 1945. On March 2, Col. George W. Coolidge of the War Department Observers Board, ETOUSA visited SUSA and was given briefings on the expedient armor kits. The commanders of both the 25th and 48th Tank battalions testified that at least eight

tanks from their units had been saved in the preceding days by the sandbag armor and that it had stopped both *Panzerfaust* and *Panzerschreck* hits. Coolidge concluded that "If the bags did nothing more, they were certainly a morale factor as the crews were thoroughly impressed with them."

In response to the interest shown by higher commands, on March 9, 1945, the 1st Armored Group decided to test the SUSA modification package using captured Panzerfaust 60 launchers. Shots from 20–30ft were aimed perpendicularly against the double layer of sandbags mounted on the hull side. These shots blasted the sandbags away from within the welded steel cages and resulted in penetrations through the sponson armor. The next tests were conducted against the hull front, firing from a 45-degree angle in an attempt to replicate the likely angle of a German soldier firing at the tank under typical battlefield conditions. These shots did not penetrate the front armor plate. The tests confirmed that the expedient sandbag armor had some defensive advantages depending on the angle and location of impact. A visiting observer team from the New Developments Division of the War Department concluded that "These tests are of course far from conclusive. The psychological value of the sandbags is the greatest value actually derived."

Another set of tests were conducted on March 12, 1945, by the 134th Armored Ordnance Maintenance Battalion of the 12th Armored Division. This time, the test targets were expanded to include M4 medium tanks fitted with spaced armor plate on the hull side as well as various sandbag configurations. The spaced armor was subjected to fire from US 76mm guns as well as 2.36in bazookas and German rocket weapons. Records of the tests, aside from some photos, do not appear to have been preserved, and the results of the tests are not known other than the fact that the spaced armor was penetrated by tank gun fire.

THE COMBATANTS

PANZERFAUST AND *PANZERSCHRECK* DEPLOYMENT

The first *Panzerfaust* batches were ordered for field trials in July 1943 and the first deliveries from HASAG were made in August 1943. Instruction brochures were published in September 1943 and the first deliveries to the Eastern Front took place in the fall of 1943. The field tests, not surprisingly, preferred the *Panzerfaust (gross)* over the *Panzerfaust (klein)* due to the former's better penetration. The first extensive combat use took place in October 1943 with about 500 expended. As the weapon became available in more substantial numbers, troop use steadily increased with about 3,800 expended in November and 20,600 in December 1943.

There was no specific *Panzerfaust* allocation in German tables of organization and equipment (KStN: Kriegsstärkenachweisungen: war establishment strength) because it was considered a disposable munition such as a grenade rather than a weapon such as a rifle. Instead, there was an allocation of *Panzerfaust* weapons as part of the unit *Ausstattung* (unit-of-fire). This was a standardized figure for the amount of munitions needed for three days of average fighting or one day of intense fighting. So for an infantry division, the *Panzerfaust* unit-of-fire was 2,000 rounds. Of this, each infantry company was nominally authorized 36 *Panzerfäuste*. Mechanized units had a smaller allotment on the grounds that they already had ample means for antitank defense. So a Panzer division had a unit-of-fire of 1,000 *Panzerfäuste* and the *Panzergrenadier* division was allotted 1,500 rounds. Besides their use in combat units, *Panzerfäuste* were widely distributed for self-defense to rear-area units such as communication and transport units, usually on a scale of 50–70 per battalion. The unit-of-fire was simply a convenient means for logistical record keeping and was not a fixed amount. So, during an operation, a unit on the fringe of the mission might be allotted a 0.5 unit-of-fire while a unit in the center of combat might be allotted 3 units-of-fire.

The Red Army did not recognize the debut of the *Panzerfaust* until late in 1943. One of the first reports of the new weapon was made in late December 1943, by the 30th Guards Rifle Corps of the 2d Ukrainian Front that reported encounters with a "rocket propelled thermite HEAT grenade" weapon. Instructions were sent out to units to encourage the capture of further examples of the weapons, and to include questions about the new weapon when interrogating German prisoners.

The delivery of the first *Panzerschreck* launchers was delayed due to problems with the rocket propellant. The first batch of weapons for troop trials was delivered on October 5, 1943, but the weapon was not officially considered to be in service until November 1943 due to the ammunition issue. In contrast to the *Panzerfaust*, the *Panzerschreck* was deployed under tables of organization and equipment as detailed below.

To speed the deployment of the new weapon to the Eastern Front, in September 1943 the Army High Command began the formation of special motorized tank-destroyer battalions – *Panzerzerstörer-Bataillone (mot.)* – for the Ostheer (Eastern Army). The first ten battalions, numbers 470 to 479, were created in September–October 1943. Six more were later formed, of which two, Panzerzerstörer-Bataillone 485 and 486, were deployed on the Western Front in the fall of 1944. Each battalion was authorized 216 *Panzerschreck* launchers, with ten rockets per launcher. The battalions were organized into three companies, each authorized 54 *Panzerschreck* launchers and 540 rockets; the remaining launchers and rockets were in battalion reserve. The original ten motorized tank-destroyer battalions were deployed at army group level in late 1943 with three each in Heeresgruppen Süd, Mitte, and Nord, and one in Heeresgruppe A. In practice, they were generally dispersed on a scale of one per field army. These could be used to rapidly create a defensive barrier against Soviet tank offensives. Owing to the shortages of the new weapon, these battalions were understrength through early 1944, with most reporting that they had less than half of their authorized 216 *Panzerschreck* launchers. In Heeresgruppe Süd in Ukraine, larger numbers of *Panzerfäuste* were issued to make up for the shortfalls. The motorized tank-destroyer battalions were not notably successful and most were disbanded during the course of 1944.

Besides the dedicated tank-destroyer units, the *Panzerschreck* was also issued to selected infantry divisions and other formations. Initially in the fall of 1943, the scale was 25 *Panzerschreck* launchers per division, and 100 per field army. As new tables of organization and equipment were gradually issued, more formal allotments began to appear. In infantry regiments, they were deployed in the Panzerjäger-Kompanie, traditionally called 14. Kompanie. This company had a platoon equipped with six 7.5cm PaK 40 antitank guns and two platoons with 18 *Panzerschreck* launchers each for a total of 36 per regiment. The fall 1944-pattern *Volksgrenadier* division dispensed with the towed antitank guns and had 72 *Panzerschreck* launchers. The modified infantry regiments in 1944–45, based on two rather than the previous three rifle battalions, had 35 *Panzerschreck* launchers in each rifle battalion and 13 in other sub-units for a total of 83 per regiment.

In the Panzer and *Panzergrenadier* divisions, the November 1943 KStN authorized each *Panzergrenadier* battalion one *Panzerschreck* per rifle squad (*Gruppe*) and four in the heavy-weapons company. Curiously enough, these disappeared from the next KStN in April 1944, presumably on the grounds that the

Panzerschreck teams assigned to some units such as Fusilier battalions were provided with bicycles for greater mobility. This is a *Panzerschreck* unit of Heeresgruppe G in France in September 1944.

Panzergrenadier regiments were already well equipped with antitank guns and the *Panzerschreck* launchers were sorely needed in regular infantry units. This policy changed again under the November 1944 KStN when each *Panzergrenadier* company was authorized a *Panzerzerstörertrupp* of seven men consisting of a troop leader and three two-man teams, each team with a *Panzerschreck* for a total of three launchers per troop.

It should be noted that there was usually a significant gap between the number of weapons authorized under the various KStN and the number of weapons actually deployed in regiments and divisions. This was especially so with a new weapon such as the *Panzerschreck*. The standard unit-of-fire for the *Panzerschreck* was ten rockets per launcher.

As in the case of the *Panzerfaust* in 1943, combat use of the *Panzerschreck* steadily increased from only about 200 rockets expended in October 1943 during the troop trials to 1,300 in November and 8,300 in December. One of the first Red Army reports on the *Panzerschreck* came in late 1943 when a German soldier was captured from 58. Infanterie-Division, 16. Armee in the Nevel region of northern Russia.

Delivery of the *Puppchen* began in November 1943, but the first extensive combat use was delayed until February 1944 due to ammunition issues. This weapon had a lower priority than the *Panzerschreck*, and there was no significant ammunition delivery until January 1944. The combat use in February 1944 totaled only about 3,500 rockets. Although sometimes issued to regular infantry units, many of the *Puppchen* seem to have been reserved for the *Fallschirmjäger* formations of the Luftwaffe.

The introduction of better infantry antitank weapons led to a sharp increase in the award of the Panzervernichtungsabzeichen decoration. At first, this award was not issued to soldiers using the *Panzerschreck* on the grounds that it was a crew-served weapon, but on December 18, 1943, the rules were changed to grant the award to successful *Panzerschreck* gunners. About 10,000 of these awards were issued from March 1942 through May 1944, and by the end of the war, some 18,451 had been issued. The pace of granting the award more than doubled in June 1944–April 1945 largely due to the

The nickname for German soldiers involved in close-combat against enemy tanks was *Panzerknacker* (Tank Cracker). This was an allusion to the popular Christmas *Nussknacker* (Nut Cracker) dolls as depicted on the cover of this field manual for close-combat against tanks.

advent of the *Panzerfaust*. Besides the basic silver award, 421 soldiers were awarded the gold insignia for the destruction of five enemy tanks. Many of the top scoring "infantry aces" won their awards with the *Panzerfaust*.

There is some dispute regarding the highest-scoring *Panzerknacker* (Tank Cracker) because comprehensive record keeping was lacking. Many assessments, compiled decades later, were based on interpretation of photos, estimating which insignia were silver or gold. For many years, Oberleutnant Günther Viezenz was considered the high scorer with 21 kills, but Viezenz himself later noted that buffs had misinterpreted a well-known photo and that in fact he was instead credited with only seven kills. As detailed on page 55, Heinrich Zubrod is now widely credited as the highest scorer, but this issue remains contentious.

The focus of the German antitank rocket launcher program was the Eastern Front. The first Allied reports of encounters with the *Panzerfaust* in the West took place in Italy during January–February 1944, several months after their debut in the East. Surviving records of the German static infantry divisions manning the Atlantic Wall on the Normandy Front at the time of D-Day reveal that these units generally were not equipped with the *Panzerfaust* or *Panzerschreck*. In contrast, the normal infantry divisions in France were equipped with the new weapons. For example, 275. Infanterie-Division, stationed in Brittany near Saint-Nazaire, had 34 *Panzerschreck* launchers in each of its three regiments for a total of 102.

In the wake of the D-Day invasion, there was an urgent call for the dispatch of modern antitank weapons to Normandy. Facing the Americans on the Cotentin Peninsula near Cherbourg and in the bocage country near Saint-Lô, 7. Armee was in a particularly desperate situation. On June 11, 1944, it sent out instructions to the four divisions in Brittany – 265., 266., and 277. Infanterie-Divisionen and 5. Fallschirmjäger-Division – to turn over 65 percent of their *Panzerschreck* launchers and *Panzerfäuste* to LXXXIV. Armeekorps, which was facing the Americans in Lower Normandy.

Having sent a *Kampfgruppe* (battlegroup) to Normandy in mid-June to support 352. Infanterie-Division, 277. Infanterie-Division issued a report by its Panzerjäger-Abteilung 275. The report noted that: "When facing tanks, fire should be withheld up to as close a range as possible so that success can be assured. The Panzerschreck and Panzerfaust have been particularly successful in country where the hedgerows obstruct visibility. Twenty-five of the tanks knocked out on the invasion front so far have been attributed to these weapons."

HEINRICH ZUBROD

Leutnant Heinrich Zubrod was probably the top *Panzerknacker* (Tank Cracker) of the Wehrmacht in World War II, and certainly the top-scoring infantryman of the ETO. Zubrod was born on November 2, 1918 in Grillsheim, Bavaria. He was drafted into the Wehrmacht on February 1, 1940. He served as an enlisted man on the Eastern Front until December 1942 when he was promoted to *Leutnant der Reserve* (lieutenant of the reserves). In the summer of 1943 he was awarded both classes of the Iron Cross in a three-week period as well as the Nahkampfspange (Close Combat Clasp) in bronze.

In late 1944, Zubrod served as a company commander in Grenadier-Regiment 1213 of 189. Infanterie-Division. The division served in Alsace in late 1944 and early 1945, fighting mainly against elements of the 1e Armée Française (1st French Army) in the Colmar pocket. In December 1944–January 1945, his company was involved in the heavy fighting around Siegoldsheimer Höhe, west of Colmar. (This area is now part of the town of Kayserberg-Vignoble.)

During this fighting, Zubrod was credited with knocking out 11 tanks with *Panzerfäuste*, four of which he knocked out in a single day. These were mostly from the French 5e Division Blindée. On January 18, 1945 he was awarded the Knight's Cross for his actions, the second member of his regiment awarded the Knight's Cross for actions around Siegoldsheimer Höhe. (Major Josef Hollermeier, the regimental commander, was awarded this decoration after he was killed in action on December 4, 1944.) Zubrod

appeared in a news clip of the popular newsreel *Deutsche Wochenschau* (The German Weekly Review) in its January 18, 1945 edition, explaining his exploits with the *Panzerfaust*. Over the following days, he knocked out two more tanks, bringing his total to 13. Zubrod was killed in action near Munzenheim in January 1945 during the fighting for the left bank of the Rhine River.

GERMAN FORCES AT VILLIERS-FOSSARD

The German units involved in the June 29–30 Villiers-Fossard fighting examined in this study were from 352. Infanterie-Division. This division had defended Omaha Beach on D-Day, and had fought against the 29th Infantry Division for the previous two weeks. During this fighting, the division suffered casualties of 5,407, in effect its entire combat strength. The intention had been to pull the division out of the line on June 15, 1944 and to transfer it to southern France to be rebuilt. As a result, its four replacement battalions, equivalent to about one-third of needed replacements, were diverted to camps in southern France near Montpellier awaiting the division's arrival. In the event, the division was not withdrawn due to the desperate shortage of infantry divisions in Normandy.

By late June 1944, 352. Infanterie-Division had been reduced to a combat strength of about 2,000 men, with the troops from its usual three regiments consolidated into a single regiment, Grenadier-Regiment 916. To keep the division in the line, it was reinforced by battlegroups taken from other infantry divisions, mainly from those that were idle in Brittany. As a result, at the end of June the division had a combat strength of 5,480 men as detailed below. Combat strength (*Kampfstärke*) only included the troops in forward combat units who constituted about 45 percent of the total division strength (*Iststärke*). So total divisional strength of 352. Infanterie-Division at this time may have been about 12,000 men.

Units under command of 352. Infanterie Division, June 29, 1944

Unit	Origins	Combat strength
KG *Goth*	Grenadier-Regiment 916 (352. Infanterie-Division)	2,000
KG *Kentner*	Grenadier-Regiment 897 (266. Infanterie-Division)	1,800
KG *Böhm*	II. Bataillon, Grenadier-Regiment 943 and Füsilier-Bataillon 353 (353. Infanterie-Division)	980
Reserve I	Schnelle-Brigade 30	200
Reserve II	II. Bataillon, Grenadier-Regiment 898 (343. Infanterie-Division)	500
Total		*5,480*

The division held a sector roughly 6 miles wide, from the Vire River to the Elle River, with the contemporary D6 road as its eastern boundary. Its three battlegroups from west to east were KG *Kentner*, KG *Goth*, and KG *Böhm*. The Villiers-Fossard salient was held on its west flank by KG *Goth*, consisting mainly of Füsilier-Bataillon 352. The east flank of the salient was defended by KG *Böhm*. This consisted of Oberst Böhm's Grenadier-Regiment 943 (353. Infanterie-Division), minus I./GR 943. Since the regiment had only two battalions, this meant that it consisted mainly of Major Dickertmann's II./GR 943. It was further reinforced by Rittmeister Theurkauf's Füsilier-Bataillon 353. This battlegroup was the weakest of the three in the division with a combat strength of only 980 men. The remnants of Schnelle-Brigade 30, numbering 200 men, held the shoulder of the salient in the southeast.

Details of the antitank resources of these formations are lacking. 352. Infanterie-Division was equipped with the *Panzerschreck* in early 1944, probably on a scale of 36 per regiment. The heavy-weapons company of Füsilier-Bataillon 352 had three *Panzerschreck* launchers, according to a prisoner-of-war report. How many were still in use by the division on June 29 is not known. The division does not appear to have been issued *Panzerfäuste* prior to D-Day, but evidently received them subsequently as numerous examples were captured by US troops during the battle.

By the end of June 1944, the division had ample experience fighting the M4 medium tank in bocage conditions. The 29th Infantry Division was supported by the 747th Tank Battalion during the June fighting and suffered relatively high losses with 37 M4 medium tanks and 4 M5A1 light tanks lost. Details regarding the cause(s) of the losses are lacking, though the battalion after-action-report makes numerous mentions of German "bazookas."

By this stage of the campaign, 352. Infanterie-Division had well-established tactics for the bocage fighting. There was usually a thinly manned outpost line along the forward-edge-of-battle. This was followed a field or two back by the main battle line (HKL: Hauptkampflinie). The defenses were dug into the base of the hedgerows, usually with a machine-gun position and an antitank position in each corner. Riflemen were located along the hedgerow, almost invariably dug in to a protected firing position. Each hedgerow "box" was defended by a force ranging from a squad (*Gruppe*) to a platoon (*Zug*) depending on the local circumstances. There was generally one or more *Panzerfäuste* covering each box, with *Panzerschreck* teams assigned to critical defense positions.

A German infantry platoon on the march in bocage country in the summer of 1944. The soldier third from the front is armed with a Panzerfaust 30 (gross).

The previous combat had shown the importance of artillery support in the bocage fighting. This consisted of the mortars organic to the regiments, and divisional artillery. Two battalions of Artillerie-Regiment 1352, each equipped with eight 10.5cm leFH 18 howitzers, were assigned to support KG *Goth* and KG *Kentner*. Since KG *Kentner* was relatively inactive during the June 29–30 fighting, these battalions would have been assigned to KG *Goth* and KG *Böhm*. There was also an improvised Artillerie-Abteilung *Autun* equipped with heavy field howitzers that was in direct support of the division. Shortly before the start of the fighting, a battalion of Fallschirm-Flak-Regiment 2 with three batteries of 8.8cm antiaircraft guns was also assigned to provide support against ground targets, but this was located farther south in the vicinity of Saint-Lô. Besides this substantial arsenal of field artillery, KG *Goth* had a well-established network of forward artillery observers, all linked to the divisional artillery network via field telephones. This substantially improved the lethality of the artillery available to the division.

US ARMY FORCES AT VILLIERS-FOSSARD

The 3d Armored Division – one of two "heavy" armored divisions in the ETO that followed the older 1942 "heavy" table of organization – arrived in France starting on June 23, 1944. The other "heavy" division in the ETO was the 2d Armored Division. As a result, these divisions were each based around two armored regiments and one armored infantry regiment. The 1942 configuration was tank-

An M4 medium tank knocked out by *Panzerfaust* strikes during the fighting around Villiers-Fossard. This was probably a tank from Co. B, 747th Tank Battalion because Co. B, 32d Armored Regiment was equipped with M5A1 light tanks. The 747th Tank Battalion lost several of its tanks to *Panzerfaust* hits during the fighting northwest of Villiers-Fossard in the third week of June.

heavy and infantry-poor, with six tank battalions and three armored infantry battalions compared to the 1943 "light" pattern of three tank battalions and three armored infantry battalions. The 3d Armored Division was extremely well trained but had no practical battle experience. Villiers-Fossard was to be its first taste of combat.

The XIX Corps field orders directed the division to attack with CCA. This was a combined-arms formation mixing various component elements from the division to create a balanced team. The principal combat units assigned to CCA were the 32d Armored Regiment, 36th Armored Infantry Regiment, 803d Tank Destroyer Battalion, and 23d Armored Engineer Battalion. CCA was divided into three task forces as detailed below. In turn, each task force was usually subdivided into two assault groups, led by one of the tank or armored infantry battalion commanders. Typically, these would consist of one tank company, one armored infantry company, and a supporting engineer squad; the remaining companies of the battalions would then constitute a reserve.

CCA, Brig. Gen. Doyle O. Hickey, June 29, 1944

TF X (Col. Truman E. Boudinot): 3/32d Armored Regiment (Lt. Col. Walter B. Richardson); 3/36th Armored Infantry Regiment (Lt. Col. Carlton P. Russell); Co. A, 803d Tank Destroyer Battalion; Co. C, 23d Armored Engineer Battalion.

TF Y (Col. Graeme G. Parks): 2d Battalion, 32d Armored Regiment (Lt. Col. Nathaniel O. Whitlaw); 2d Battalion, 36th Armored Infantry Regiment (Lt. Col. Vincent E. Cockefair); Co. B, 803d Tank Destroyer Battalion; Co. A, 23d Armored Engineer Battalion.

TF Z (Lt. Col. Walter Abney): 1st Battalion, 32d Armored Regiment (Lt. Col. Elwyn W. Blanchard); 1st Battalion, 36th Armored Infantry Regiment (Lt. Col. William R. Orr); Co. C, 803d Tank Destroyer Battalion; Co. B, 23d Armored Engineer Battalion.

LAFAYETTE POOL

Lafayette G. Pool was born on July 23, 1919 in Odem, Texas and was drafted into the United States Army on June 14, 1941. He was assigned to the new 3d Armored Division and was promoted to staff sergeant in 1943 when the unit was deployed to Britain. His tank, named "In the Mood," was assigned to the 3d Platoon, Co. I, 32d Armored Regiment, 3d Armored Division and took part in the fighting for Villiers-Fossard as part of TF X. His first tank was knocked out by a *Panzerfaust* or *Panzerschreck* strike around 1150hrs on June 29, 1944 during the fighting near Belle Fontaine; the crew escaped. He later recalled: "My tank was knocked out by bazooka fire – four shots glanced off, one penetrated. The ones that glanced off were fired at a range greater than 50 yards. The one that penetrated was about 20 yards. I think, therefore, that the enemy bazooka is effective only at close range."

Pool went on to become one of the top-scoring tank aces of the US Army in Normandy, credited with 12 tank kills and 258 other vehicles. His second tank was the victim of a friendly fire attack by a P-38 Lightning fighter-bomber near Fromental, France on August 17. His third tank, an M4A1 (76mm), was knocked out by a Panther tank of 9. Panzer-Division on the evening of September 15, 1944 during fighting near Munsterbusch, Germany, southwest of Aachen. Pool suffered severe injuries and had his right leg amputated after the engagement. He was highly decorated for his leadership including the Distinguished Service Cross, Legion of Merit, Silver Star, Purple Heart, the Belgian Fourragère, and the French Légion d'Honneur. He returned to the United States and retired from the US Army on September 19, 1960 with the rank of chief warrant officer second class. Pool's exploits helped inspire the 1951 motion picture *The Tanks are Coming*. Pool was sometimes called "War Daddy," a name that was later used for the tank commander played by Brad Pitt in the 2014 film *Fury*. Pool died on May 30, 1991.

The mission plan positioned TF Y to attack directly into the Villiers-Fossard salient while TF X pushed against the eastern shoulder of the salient. TF Z was the mission reserve and positioned between the other two task forces.

In terms of force ratios, the German defenders had a marked advantage in infantry with the force ratio being about 2:3 in the German favor. It should be recalled that the usual rule-of-thumb for a successful attack was a 3:1 advantage in favor of the attacker. The German side had only a handful of armored vehicles while CCA had about 115 M4 medium tanks, 70 M5A1 light tanks, and about 30 M10 3in GMC tank destroyers. The US side also had a decided advantage in artillery, about 16 battalions versus about five German battalions.

THE STRATEGIC SITUATION

The focus of this study is the two-day battle around the small village of Villiers-Fossard in Normandy on June 29–30 between 352. Infanterie-Division and CCA, 3d Armored Division. By late June 1944, 352. Infanterie-Division had few surviving antitank guns, and so relied very heavily on the *Panzerfaust* and *Panzerschreck* for antitank defense. These weapons proved to be extremely deadly due to the nature of the local bocage terrain.

The US Army's 29th Infantry Division attempted to secure the approaches to the vital crossroads town of Saint-Lô during the second and third week of June 1944. This area was dominated by bocage terrain. From a defensive standpoint, the dense hedgerows that edged the farm fields formed an inverted trench system. The German forces exploited the defensive value of these natural terrain features, successfully impeding the American attacks.

By the third week of June 1944, the 29th Infantry Division had reached to within 4.5 miles of Saint-Lô. The German defenses around Villiers-Fossard had proven to be unusually resistant to attack. The division's 115th Infantry Regiment, supported by the 747th Tank Battalion, had made a final unsuccessful attempt to capture the village on June 21. After two weeks of fighting against 352. Infanterie-Division, however, the 29th Infantry Division was exhausted and had suffered too many casualties to continue the fight. As a result, the Villiers-Fossard salient remained in this sector, projecting northward into American lines.

In late June 1944, the US Army's XIX Corps wanted the Villiers-Fossard salient reduced prior to the renewal of the Saint-Lô offensive that was scheduled for early July 1944. XIX Corps chose to employ the corps reserve, the newly arrived CCA

3d Armored Division in what was considered to be a limited action, expected to take about a day. The use of an armored division to conduct a breakthrough attack of this type was against doctrine, which envisioned the armored division as an exploitation force once the breakthrough had been secured by the infantry. In spite of this, XIX Corps felt that it would be worthwhile for the 3d Armored Division to gain some combat experience. Intelligence assessments of the German forces in the salient were poor, and it was expected that the attack would only face a modest defense force made up of a few German *Ersatz* (replacement) infantry battalions.

By the time of the battle for Villiers-Fossard, the *Panzerfaust* had begun to be issued in large numbers to German units in Normandy. This is a Panzerfaust 30 (gross) cache found near Villiers-Fossard after the battle for the village.

THE TERRAIN

The bocage terrain was better suited to defense than to offense and in effect constituted a series of compartmented defense works. The terrain was especially unsuited to tank operation because the hedgerows were too tall to be easily overcome by tanks. Those tanks that did try to drive over hedgerows exposed their thin bellies to German antitank rocket or gun attack. The S-3 operations officer for TF Y, Maj. James Bryan, later described the consequences of the terrain on the operation:

> This type of terrain gave great advantage to the defender. With the summer foliage on the trees and bushes and the high grass growing on the hedgerows, visibility was limited in a great number of cases to the field immediately beyond the observer. High ground did not have the key importance it would normally merit. However, it was still of great importance in that an observer on high ground could have a commanding view of the road network.

Besides limiting observations, the hedgerows themselves were a barrier to movement of vehicles and personnel. Some were not as thick or high as others, but almost all of them were sufficiently large to cause difficulty in movement. They were from six to ten feet thick at the base and from four to eight feet in height. Out of the earth of the rows, bushes and trees grew. Some of the trees were full grown, ten to twelve inches in diameter or larger. The sod had been packed down year after year and the stumps of old trees, roots of trees, and other growth had made them a solid composition which made them difficult to tear down.

With a minimum of work, the enemy could use these barriers to gain the best type of cover and concealment. A hole dug out of the bank made a shelter from practically all types of fire. A slit through the bank made a firing aperture which afforded protection for the firer. A little digging provided a protected platform for a machine gun, and mortars could be emplaced so that the crews and weapons were rendered less vulnerable to artillery or small arms fire.

The terrain around Villiers-Fossard was dominated by hedgerows, evident in this view from a German observation post north of the village, looking in the direction of the American attack on June 29, 1944.

CCA was aware of the unique challenges posed by the bocage terrain and attempted to develop tactics to employ tanks effectively in these constrained conditions. They discussed previous missions with troops from the 115th Infantry Regiment (29th Infantry Division) as well as the 747th Tank Battalion. A key aspect of bocage

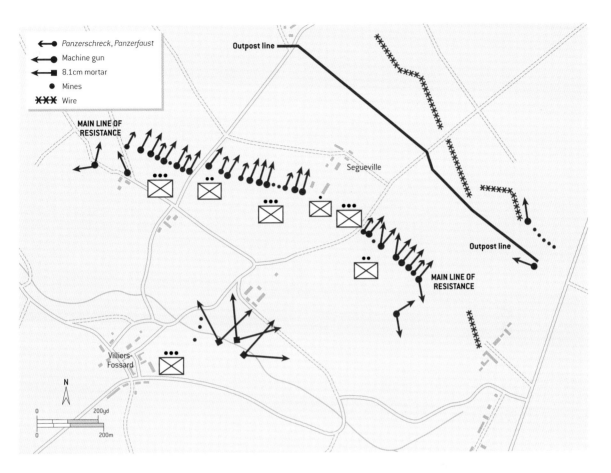

The defense of Villiers-Fossard by Füsilier-Bataillon 353, KG *Böhm*.

fighting was to develop some method to penetrate the compartmented fields. The two most promising techniques involved the use of tank dozers and engineer explosive charges. Tank dozers could clear a path through a hedgerow that was wide enough for other tanks and accompanying infantry to follow. The main problem was a shortage of these relatively new vehicles – there were only eight available – and so they were divided between the two attack task forces. Engineer explosive charges were an alternative, but they took considerable time to emplace. As a result, this method of breaching the hedgerows served as a back-up.

The tactics for the Villiers-Fossard mission involved the use of combined-arms breaching teams, each team based around a platoon of five M4 medium tanks and a platoon of dismounted armored infantry. They were supported by engineer squads and a tank-destroyer platoon operating in an overwatch position. Each infantry–tank team was separated from its neighbors by one hedgerow-edged field. The attack began with a tank dozer plowing an opening into the next field, after which the infantry–tank team would pour through the gap. In view of the *Panzerfaust* threat, the tanks were supposed to remain no closer than 50yd to any of the hedgerows, with a screen of infantry to deal with the *Panzerfaust* threat. Once a field had been secured, the infantry–tank team would clear the field to its right and left in conjunction with neighboring infantry–tank teams. Once this was accomplished, the process would be repeated toward the next set of fields. The plan was to deliberately grind through the hedgerows.

COMBAT

VILLIERS-FOSSARD, JUNE 29

The June 29 attack on the Villiers-Fossard salient was scheduled to begin with an attack by USAAF fighter-bombers starting at 0825hrs, lasting for about 15 minutes. In the event, there was light rain that morning and the cloud cover led to the cancellation of air support. Artillery fire from the divisional artillery and supporting corps artillery began at 0840hrs, lasting about 5 minutes. This was followed by rifle and heavy-weapons fire along the forward edge of the battle area, lasting from 0845hrs to 0850hrs. This in turn was followed by 10 minutes of artillery fire.

KG *Goth* heard the approaching USAAF aircraft around 0820hrs, and presumed that it signaled an air and artillery attack. The experienced German troops had learned that the best way to avoid the bombardment phase was to infiltrate forward, as close to the American start positions as possible, since the Americans invariably left a significant safety margin between the forward edge of troops and the bombardment. As a result, German casualties during the pre-attack bombardment were light. Furthermore, the hedgerows absorbed most of the punishment from the artillery bombardment with little harm to the scattered earthen emplacements. By the time the US attack began, the German troops had returned to their combat positions.

TF X began its attack southward at 0900hrs. The lead elements were soon brought under intense German mortar fire. Around 1100hrs, troops spotted a German forward observer in a tree overlooking the area, and after he was killed, the mortar fire diminished in accuracy and intensity. The main German resistance centered around the hamlet of La Fossardière. TF X reached Phase Line 1, the road from La Forge to Bois de Brétel; around 1300hrs they were ordered to halt for about 2 hours because the attack by TF Y had been held up by German resistance. During this interlude, TF X was subjected to heavy mortar and artillery fire.

The TF Y attack was bifurcated into two assault groups led by Lt. Col. Nathaniel O. Whitlaw on the left (east) and Lt. Col. Vincent E. Cockefair on the right (west). Both assault groups penetrated the German outpost line, but the Cockefair Group was held up by extremely intense mortar and artillery fire from KG *Goth*. The Whitlaw Group advanced deeper before encountering the main defenses of KG *Böhm* in the hedgerows on either side of the hamlet of Segueville around 1100hrs. An artillery barrage was requested, but the interlude between the lifting of the barrage and the advance of the infantry–tank team was too great. Again, the Germans repulsed the attack with a heavy stream of machine-gun and *Panzerfaust* fire. Another barrage was requested, but this time, the infantry–tank teams followed the cessation of the barrage much more closely. This change enabled the infantry–tank teams to break through the German main defense line, but it took another 2 hours to grind through the hedgerows to the German reserve defense line, along the Jouenne creek immediately to the east of the village of Villiers-Fossard around 1300hrs. The assault group's two tank dozers suffered mechanical breakdowns while trying to move through the swampy terrain near the creek. Whitlaw was instructed to halt the advance because Cockefair's assault group was still being held up near the line-of-departure.

The delays on the western side of the advance led to a meeting of the senior division commanders to discuss possible options. Lt. Col. William R. Orr's assault group, consisting of a company of infantry, a company of tanks, and supporting troops, was shifted from the reserve TF Z to Cockefair's assault group to reinforce the attack. Following an artillery barrage on the German positions, Cockefair's assault group began to attack at 1430hrs. The reinforced attack overwhelmed KG *Goth*'s defense line and steadily ground through the hedgerows, reaching the Jouenne creek northwest of Villiers-Fossard, and pushing across it around 1755hrs. The attack continued to the west of Villiers-Fossard, and the village was cleared by US infantry following an artillery barrage around 1930hrs. By this stage, KG *Böhm* had recognized that defense of Villiers-Fossard had become untenable, the surviving German troops having been authorized to withdraw before the American troops reached the village. Once the US infantry had moved through Villiers-Fossard, the village was bombarded again, this time by German artillery, resulting in significant US casualties. Both the Whitlaw and Cockefair assault groups were instructed to cease their advance and take up defensive positions at dusk, around 2130hrs. In fact, both assault groups continued to attack until dark, around 2245hrs, since it took time to break off the engagement.

Once TF Y had resumed its advance, TF X was instructed to resume its attack around 1500hrs. By this time, the defenses in this sector had been reinforced by Fallschirm-Aufklärungs-Abteilung 12, the reconnaissance battalion of II. Fallschirmkorps. The German mortar fire was so intense that TF X made little headway. A second push began around 1900hrs and reached as far as the orchard west of La Belle Fontaine. However, CCA headquarters instructed TF X to withdraw back to Phase Line 1 along the La Forge–Bois de Brétel road for fear of leaving an exposed western flank.

OVERLEAF
Panzerfaust ambush, Villiers-Fossard, June 29, 1944.

65

VILLIERS-FOSSARD, JUNE 30

The American attack resumed around 0800hrs on June 30. The tanks in TF X were hit by a flurry of antitank rockets and antitank gun fire around 1045hrs as they advanced across a relatively open field. Four M4 medium tanks were knocked out in quick succession. This was followed around 1315hrs by a German counterattack consisting of a few "tanks" and about two infantry platoons. The "tanks" were most likely StuG III assault guns from Fallschirm-Sturmgeschütz-Brigade 12, attached to II. Fallschirmkorps, while the troops were probably from Fallschirm-Aufklärungs-Abteilung 12. One of the StuG III was hit by an M10 3in GMC of the 803d Tank Destroyer Battalion, but the round failed to stop the German vehicle. In the event, the StuG III and an accompanying armored car turned around and withdrew. TF X suffered so many tank casualties to gunfire and *Panzerfäuste* that the US attack was put on hold along the La Forge–Bois de Brétel road.

The attack by TF Y on June 30 was complicated by the fact that the previous evening Whitlaw's assault group had slipped farther west than planned and inadvertently had wandered into the sector in front of Cockefair's assault group. To straighten out this situation, Brig. Gen. Doyle O. Hickey instructed TF Z to send an assault group under Lt. Col. Elwyn W. Blanchard alongside Whitlaw and to proceed southward. Whitlaw's assault group was instructed to remain in place until Cockefair's assault group advanced abreast. In contrast to the first day of the attack, Cockefair's assault group advanced steadily on the morning of June 30, came abreast of Whitlaw's assault group, and then the entire TF Y continued the attack southward in unison.

By this stage, KG *Böhm* had been largely destroyed in the previous day's fighting.

An M4 medium tank lost near Villiers-Fossard. Two penetrations can be seen on the hull side with the characteristic circular spall patterns of a shaped-charge detonation.

KG *Goth* withdrew to the area around Le Bourg d'Enfer and tried to set up a new defense line along the creek north of the hamlet. The new defense line was reinforced by the divisional reserve, about 500 troops from II./GR 898. Cockefair's assault group advanced over the creek farther north without encountering the new German defense line.

Around 1500hrs, TF Y was ordered by CCA to halt the advance and take up defensive positions. By this stage, the Villiers-Fossard salient had been eliminated and the mission accomplished. During the

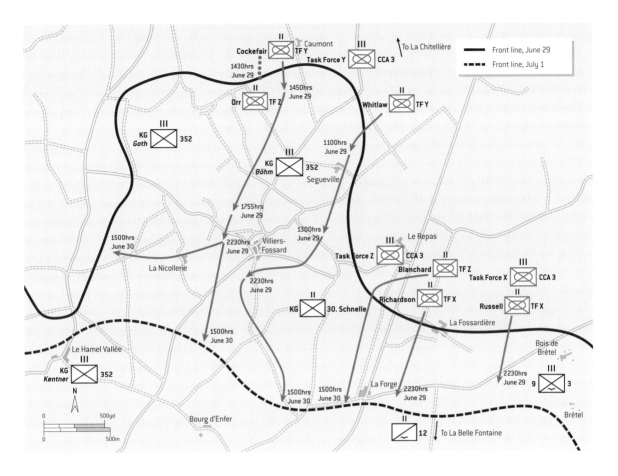

The battle of Villiers-Fossard, June 29–30, 1944.

evening, the new front line was taken over by the 29th Infantry Division, and CCA returned northward to bivouac positions around Saint-Clair-sur-l'Elle.

Assessments of the reduction of the Villiers-Fossard salient have been critical of the cost of the operation. US casualties were 384, as detailed in the accompanying table. The casualties fell most heavily on the armored infantry (301) and tankers (70). A later study of the casualties concluded that about 70 percent were from shell fragments, mainly from mortar strikes.

	US casualties, June 29–30, 1944									
Unit	June 29			June 30			Totals			Total
	KIA	MIA	WIA	KIA	MIA	WIA	KIA	MIA	WIA	
TF X	13	0	99	7	2	56	20	2	155	*177*
TF Y	24	2	81	6	0	52	30	2	133	*165*
TF Z	0	0	0	1	0	21	1	0	21	*22*
CCA	1	0	11	1	0	7	2	0	18	*20*
Total	*38*	*2*	*191*	*15*	*2*	*136*	*53*	*4*	*327*	**384**

The scale of tank losses at Villiers-Fossard has been the source of significant controversy and confusion. A XIX Corps report stated that CCA suffered 31 tanks losses on June 29–30. However, this widely repeated report was based on incomplete unit-strength reports rather than actual casualty figures. A detailed CCA casualty report from July 1, 1944 indicates that actual tank casualties were 18 M4 medium tanks and 3 M5A1 light tanks of which eight M4s and one M5A1 were total losses; the remaining 12 were knocked out but recovered. Of the M4 medium tanks where the cause of loss was identified, nine were knocked out by *Panzerfaust* or *Panzerschreck* strikes (75 percent), two by antitank guns (17 percent), and one by mortar fire (8 percent). The M5A1 light tanks were knocked out by mines.

An M4 medium tank of the 3d Platoon, Co. I, 32d Armored Regiment, TF X during the fighting at Villiers-Fossard on June 29, 1944.

There are no German casualty figures for the fighting at Villiers-Fossard except for an acknowledgment in the divisional history that losses in KG *Böhm* had been heavy. Within a few days, 7. Armee was obliged to shift another infantry regiment to 352. Infanterie-Division to keep it in the line. Another indication of the severity of German losses was the loss of German field guns to American counter-battery fire. A total of four 10.5cm leFH 18 and three 15cm sFH howitzers were lost, about one-third of the divisional strength.

The main tactical problem facing CCA at Villiers-Fossard was the clear imbalance in tank and infantry when fighting in the bocage terrain. The significant American superiority in tank strength did not translate directly into effective combat power since tank use was badly constricted by the hedgerows. In contrast, the after-action reports were unanimous in their assertion that there was simply not enough infantry to conduct such an operation in hedgerow country.

In regard to the threat posed by the German *Panzerfaust* and *Panzerschreck*, a later report noted that Whitlaw's assault group suffered fewer tank casualties than other units because the tanks from Co. E and Co. F, 32d Armored Regiment, were instructed to stay clear of the hedgerows by 50yd to reduce their vulnerability to the German antitank teams. Some of the tankers noted that they were engaged by *Panzerfäuste* from ranges as far as 50yd, but that the weapons only seemed effective at a closer range of about 20yd.

Although well trained, the 3d Armored Division was completely inexperienced at the start of the Villiers-Fossard engagement. Lt. Col. Walter B. Richardson, an assault-group commander with TF X, later remarked that the personnel of 3d Armored Division learned more during the short fight at Villiers-Fossard than they had in the previous two years of training.

ANALYSIS

The fighting for Villiers-Fossard is illustrative of the important impact of the *Panzerfaust* and *Panzerschreck* on infantry combat. Although these weapons were by no means decisive in reversing the tank threat against German infantry, they certainly helped to restore the balance in some tactical circumstances. A German infantry regiment in mid-1943 was defended by only 12 7.5cm PaK 40 antitank guns; by the summer of 1944, there were an additional 36 *Panzerschreck* launchers and as many as 500 *Panzerfäuste* per regiment. Owing to their limited range, the shaped-charge weapons were less effective than antitank guns against tanks in open country, such as in many areas of the Eastern Front. In close terrain, such as bocage, forests, or urban environments, however, the *Panzerfaust* and *Panzerschreck* posed a significant threat to tanks.

There are no comprehensive statistics regarding the causes of US tank casualties in Normandy in June–August 1944. However, a partial survey conducted by FUSA of 236 tanks knocked out in June–August 1944 indicated that, overall, 38 (16 percent) had been knocked out by *Panzerfaust* or *Panzerschreck* strikes. The casualties were notably higher during the bocage fighting in June–July when *Panzerfaust* or *Panzerschreck* strikes accounted for about 30 percent of the tanks knocked out, while they only accounted for about 5 percent of the tank casualties during the pursuit phase in August 1944. As mentioned previously, *Panzerfaust* or *Panzerschreck* strikes probably accounted for about 70 percent of the US tank casualties during the Villiers-Fossard engagement – significantly higher than average during this phase of the war.

A notable trend in the overall impact of the *Panzerfaust* and *Panzerschreck* in 1944–45 was the growing proportion of Allied tank losses attributable to these weapons in the final months of the war. This was due in no small measure to the increasing number of available weapons. In November 1943, only about 14,000 shaped-charge

German combat expenditure of shaped-charge weapons, October 1943–November 1944*

	Oct 1943	Nov 1943	Dec 1943	Jan 1944	Feb 1944	Mar 1944	Apr 1944	
Panzerschreck	0.2	1.3	8.3	1.5	23.3	20.0	57.4	
Puppchen	0	0	0	0	3.5	3.5	1.0	
Panzerfaust	0.5	3.8	20.6	8.5	33.2	109.0	32.3	
HH.3	7.4	8.9	5.0	11.6	7.2	5.8	8.1	
Total	8.1	14.0	33.9	21.6	67.2	138.3	98.8	

	May 1944	Jun 1944	Jul 1944	Aug 1944	Sep 1944	Oct 1944	Nov 1944	Total
Panzerschreck	75.0	75.0	80.0	336.0	25.0	55.0	50.0	808.0
Puppchen	1.0	6.0	15.0	35.0	7.0	9.0	0	81.0
Panzerfaust	50.0	50.0	200.0	318.0	220.0	200.0	180.0	1,425.9
HH.3	5.3	12.7	13.0	36.0	15.0	25.0	30.0	191.0
Total	131.3	143.7	308.0	725.0	267.0	289.0	260.0	**2,505.9**

*in thousands

weapons were expended by the Wehrmacht while a year later, the expenditure rate had climbed nearly twenty-fold to 260,000. This was made possible by the tremendous increase in production of these weapons in 1944. So for example, the *Panzerfaust* inventory in November 1943 was only 34,000 but a year later the stockpile was nearly fifty times greater with 1,676,100 weapons on hand.

The effect of the proliferation of these weapons was evident in the case of British Army tank casualties in Normandy to German rocket weapons. Although the losses were lower than those suffered by the US Army, this was due in no small measure to the more open terrain in the Caen area which did not facilitate the German use of their close-range weapons. This pattern remained the case in the fall and winter of 1944–45. The situation changed dramatically from late March 1945 through the end of the war in Europe, a period when shaped-charge weapons accounted for about one-third of British tank casualties. This was attributed to several factors including the growing proliferation of *Panzerfäuste* in the final months of the war, operations in forested and urban areas of Germany that facilitated German use of rocket weapons, and the sharp decline in the number of German tanks and conventional antitank guns in the final months of the war.

Percentage of British tanks lost to *Panzerfaust* and *Panzerschreck* strikes

Campaign	Tanks knocked out	Knocked out by shaped charge	Percentage of losses
Normandy (June–September 1944)	83	5	6%
Belgium and Holland (September 1944–February 8, 1945)	76	7	9%
Germany, west of the Rhine (February 8–March 24, 1945)	30	2	7%
Germany, east of the Rhine (March 24–May 3, 1945)	274	94	34%

Allied tank casualties in the ETO caused by *Panzerfaust* and *Panzerschreck* strikes 1944–45											
Jun 1944	Jul 1944	Aug 1944	Sep 1944	Oct 1944	Nov 1944	Dec 1944	Jan 1945	Feb 1945	Mar 1945	Apr 1945	May 1945
10%	22%	12%	8%	13%	8%	13%	6%	4%	15%	24%	41%

An assessment (above) of overall Allied tank casualties in the ETO conducted by the Operations Research Office at Johns Hopkins University in 1951 provides further evidence of this trend.

The percentage of tank casualties attributed to *Panzerfaust* and *Panzerschreck* strikes in 1944–45 varied somewhat from army to army and theater to theater, as noted in the table below. Losses in the Italian theater averaged about 6 percent per month for most of 1944 and early 1945, peaking at around 25 percent in the final months of fighting beyond the Po River. This was a lower percentage of overall losses than in the campaign in Northwest Europe where loss rates were consistently higher.

Tank casualties to *Panzerfaust* by army/theater 1944–45 (percent)		1944	1945	Average
Italy	US	2.9%	18.2%	6.8%
	UK	9.0%	12.2%	9.5%
	Canada	2.0%	15.4%	2.4%
ETO	US	11.7%	11.4%	11.9%
	UK	12.7%	21.4%	15.3%
	Canada	4.8%	10.6%	7.7%

An M4A3 of NUSA's 743d Tank Battalion is gingerly driven down to the shore of the Rhine River to board a pontoon ferry for the crossing of the river on March 24, 1945. This tank has an unusual appliqué of sand-filled steel ammunition boxes on the hull side for protection against *Panzerfaust* strikes.

Although the percentage of tank casualties caused by the *Panzerfaust* and *Panzerschreck* was generally lower than losses to antitank guns and tank gun fire, British and Canadian tankers noted that these new infantry weapons had effects far beyond the statistical loss rate. Owing to the growing number of casualties to these weapons, especially in towns and forests, tank units tended to act much more cautiously due to the *Panzerfaust* threat. In addition, the pace of operations was often slowed because tank units would halt outside towns and forests to await the arrival of accompanying infantry that was needed to reduce the chance of tank losses to *Panzerfaust* strikes.

THE RED ARMY EXPERIENCE

Generaloberst Heinz Guderian's Generalinspekteur der Panzerwaffe headquarters prepared a report in the spring of 1944 identifying the types of weapons credited with the destruction of Soviet tanks and AFVs where known. As can be seen in the accompanying table, close-combat weapons were the least significant source of Soviet AFV casualties, amounting to only about 6 percent of the claims. Of the 520 AFVs claimed by close-combat weapons, the *Panzerfaust* was by far the most effective with 265 kills (51 percent), while the *Panzerschreck* was credited with 88 (17 percent). The other major tank killers were 78 kills (15 percent) by hand-emplaced antitank mines and 68 kills (13 percent) by HH.3 magnetic antitank grenades. In terms of effectiveness per expended munition, the hand-emplaced magnetic antitank grenade remained the most effective, but it was also the least widely employed due to the high degree of risk associated with its use. The *Panzerfaust* had nearly double the effectiveness of the *Panzerschreck*, probably due to its much larger and more powerful warhead.

Guderian's statistics cover only the early phase of *Panzerfaust* deployment on the Eastern Front when the weapons were still relatively few in number. Unfortunately, no comprehensive statistics on Red Army losses to *Panzerfaust* and *Panzerschreck* strikes later in 1944 have yet been discovered, though they may very well exist somewhere deep in the Russian archives. Soviet historical accounts usually lump *Panzerfaust* and *Panzerschreck* casualties together under the rubric of *Faustpatronen*. One study examined the density of German antitank defenses in several of the final campaigns and shows the growing proliferation of *Panzerfäuste* and *Panzerschreck* launchers in the final months of the war.

Soviet tank/AFV kill claims made by the Wehrmacht, January–April 1944					
	January	**February**	**March**	**April**	**Total**
Soviet AFVs destroyed	4,727	2,273	2,663	2,878	*12,541*
German weapon known	3,670	1,905	1,031	1,542	*8,148*
Weapon not known	1,057	368	1,632	1,336	*4,393*
By tank	1,401 (38%)	853 (45%)	122 (12%)	820 (53%)	*3,196 (39%)*
By *Sturmgeschütz* or *Panzerjäger*	757 (21%)	427 (22%)	297 (29%)	236 (15%)	*1,717 (21%)*
By antitank gun	1,050 (29%)	341 (18%)	327 (32%)	251 (16%)	*1,969 (24%)*
By artillery or mines	348 (9%)	148 (8%)	142 (14%)	63 (4%)	*701 (9%)*
By close-combat weapon	114 (3%)	91 (5%)	143 (14%)	172 (11%)	*520 (6%)*

Munitions per tank/AFV kill, January–April 1944			
Weapon	**Rounds expended**	**Kills**	**Rounds per kill**
Panzerfaust	183,000	265	691
Panzerschreck	102,200	88	1,161
HH.3	32,700	68	481

German antitank defense density in the East, 1944–45			
Campaign	Date	Soviet Front	*Faustpatronen* per kilometer
Umansk–Botoshansk	March 5–April 17, 1944	2d Ukrainian	6.4
Lvov–Sandomierz	July 13–August 29, 1944	1st Ukrainian	8
Vistula–Oder	January 12–February 3, 1945	1st Belorussian	87
Vistula–Oder	January 12–February 3, 1945	1st Ukrainian	100
East Prussia	January 13–April 25, 1945	1st Baltic	60
Berlin	April 16–-May 8, 1945	1st Belorussian	200

There are some snippets from Soviet unit histories that help provide some detail. The 1st Guards Tank Army suffered 92 total tank and AFV losses during the January 15–February 18, 1945 offensive of which 30 percent were attributed to *Panzerfaust* strikes. In contrast, a survey of 75 tanks and AFVs knocked out between April 16 and April 22, 1945 found that only 5 (6.6 percent) could be attributed to *Panzerfäuste*. During the Berlin operation, a survey of 33 tanks knocked out found that 12 (36 percent) had been knocked out by *Panzerfaust* strikes. A survey by the 2d Guards Tank Army found that of the 576 tanks and AFVs knocked out in the Berlin operation, 106 (18.4 percent) had been knocked out by *Panzerfäuste*. Of these, 289 were T-34 medium tanks and 65 of these T-34 casualties (22.5 percent) had been knocked out by *Panzerfäuste*.

A May 1945 report by the Armored and Mechanized Forces Directorate of the Red Army took a comprehensive look at Red Army tank losses in March 1945 and determined that of the 7,092 knocked out or disabled that month, 181 (2.5 percent) had been knocked out by *Panzerschreck* strikes. These statistics suggest much the same pattern as in the ETO, with a rise in casualties as a result of *Panzerfaust* strikes in 1945 due to their growing proliferation, and a notable increase in casualties in urban fighting compared to fighting in open terrain.

Although the Red Army continued to rely on antitank rifles through 1945, large numbers of *Panzerfäuste* were captured and also put into use. The Red Army published a manual on the use of German close-combat weapons in 1944, and distributed a Russian-language instruction booklet on the operation of the *Panzerfaust* in 1945. As well as antitank defense, the *Panzerfaust* was frequently used by Red Army units as an assault weapon, with many being issued to special assault groups of engineers during urban fighting.

While steel-reinforced concrete is denser than sandbags, it was no guarantee against shaped-charge warheads. This is an example of a 12th Armored Division M4A3E8 with concrete side armor that was hit and penetrated by a *Panzerfaust* or *Panzerschreck* projectile in 1945.

AFTERMATH

The *Panzerfaust* was the ancestor of many infantry antitank weapons that appeared after World War II. Its principal influence was in popularizing the idea of a simple, lightweight weapon that could be operated by a single soldier. In many cases, the idea of a disposable weapon lost favor, with many armies preferring to move in the direction of a reusable launcher as envisioned by the Panzerfaust 150 and Panzerfaust 250.

The most direct legacy of the *Panzerfaust* was Soviet antitank launchers. The Red Army had begun development of a weapon similar to the *Panzerfaust*, called the RPG-1 (Ruchnoy Protivotankoviy Granatomyot: hand-held antitank grenade launcher) in 1944. This was an attempt to merge the best features of the American 2.36in bazooka and the German *Panzerfaust*. Unlike the *Panzerfaust*, the RPG-1 was based on a reusable launcher, and the projectile was rocket-propelled. Although the design was completed in late 1944, it never went into production because testing revealed that the rocket motor had poor ballistic performance and the impact fuze was unreliable.

The next design, the RPG-2, was undertaken by Arkady V. Smolyakov's team at the GSKB-30 design bureau in 1945. Although the launcher was very similar to that proposed for the RPG-1, the PG-2 projectile was clearly based on captured examples of the Panzerfaust 150 and Panzerfaust 250 projectile. The rocket propulsion of the RPG-1 was dropped in favor of a propelling charge as used in the *Panzerfaust*. The PG-2 warhead was patterned on the Panzerfaust 150 warhead, using a similar conical stamped-metal nose cone, and sharing a very similar safeing and arming system. The PG-2 grenade was smaller in diameter than the Panzerfaust 150, 80mm versus 105mm, the reduction made possible by a more efficient shaped-charge warhead design. The Panzerfaust 150 used a cup-shaped

warhead liner while the PG-2 used a cone-shaped liner. As a result, the PG-2 warhead was smaller and lighter with a respectable 180mm penetration. Since the RPG-2 launcher was reusable, the propellant charge was part of the PG-2 munition, attached behind the usual tail assembly. The RPG-2 entered production in 1949 but was not widely known until the 1960s, when it saw widespread use by Viet Cong personnel and North Vietnamese troops during the Vietnam War (1955–75). It was succeeded in 1961 by the RPG-7, a further evolution that has subsequently become the most widely used antitank rocket-propelled grenade launcher in the world.

Turning to efforts to counter shaped-charge weapons after World War II, the development of methods to defeat shaped-charge warheads continued after 1945. Today's explosive reactive armor (ERA) and active protection systems (APS) can substantially degrade the performance of weapons such as the RPG-7. What is not widely known is that both concepts were already under development in the United States and the Soviet Union in the late 1940s, though neither technology came to maturity for several decades. Passive armor solutions also date back to the late 1940s, including layered armor using ceramics and other materials. It would be interesting to test the NUSA layered expedient armor to see if NUSA might have inadvertently stumbled upon the concept of passive armor solutions decades before such systems became standard on main battle tanks. British and Canadian tests of spaced armor in 1945 eventually led to Burlington armor which has formed the basis for most new NATO tank armor since the 1970s.

Readers familiar with new styles of anti-RPG defense such as slat armor or screen armor such as Q-Net, might wonder why these are effective but their ancestors such as German mesh aprons were not. The principal reason is that modern antitank rockets such as the RPG-7 use a fundamentally different safeing and arming system than the wartime weapons. The *Panzerfaust* used a simple impact fuze to detonate the warhead. A major problem with impact fuzes was their slow reaction time. If the projectile was traveling too fast, the shaped-charge liner would be crushed on impact before the penetrating jet could form properly.

In contrast, the postwar development of piezoelectric sensors circumvented this problem because their reaction time is substantially faster. They can initiate the explosive formation of the penetrating jet much more quickly. Although piezoelectric fuzes have become the dominant variety in modern shaped-charge warheads, this feature can itself be used to defeat the warhead by capturing the nose-mounted fuze between slats or screens, preventing the fuze from making any contact with the target.

The Panzerfaust 150 remains a mystery because no examples of the launcher are known to have survived. This launcher was captured by the Red Army in 1945, but it is unclear if it was a standard-production example, or a prototype. It has an additional forward handgrip and a rear shoulder brace not found on previous *Panzerfaust* weapons.

FURTHER READING

Published accounts of the technical development of German shaped-charge antitank weapons are numerous but there has been little in-depth study of their combat use. The data here on the production and combat expenditure of these weapons comes primarily from HWA records, especially the periodic reports to the OKH entitled "Überblick uber den Rüstungsstand des Heeres" (Overview of Army Munitions Levels) found in the Records Group 242 collection at the National Archives and Records Administration II (NARA II) in College Park, Maryland.

The account of the battle of Villiers-Fossard from the American perspective is based primarily on archival records in Record Group 407 at NARA II from the Combat Interviews collection as well as after-action reports of sub-units of the 3d Armored Division. Few records of 352. Infanterie-Division survived the war, and the German side of the battle came mainly from the Foreign Military Studies account listed below.

The US Army's experiments with expedient armor in the ETO has never been comprehensively documented. The account here was pieced together using a wide range of archival reports, primarily from the records of various armored groups, armored sections, AFV & W Sections and AGF Observers teams of the US Army in the ETO in Record Groups 165 and 407 at NARA II.

US GOVERNMENT REPORTS

Bryan, James (1949). *The Operations of Task Force "Y", Combat Command A (3rd Armored Division) at Villiers-Fossard, France, 29–30 June 1944.* Fort Benning, GA: Infantry School.

Coox, Alvin & L. Van Loan Naisawald (1951). *Survey of Allied Tank Casualties in World War II.* Operations Research Office, Johns Hopkins University, MD.

Gee, H.G. (1950). *The Comparative Performance of German Anti-Tank Weapons during World War II.* Army Operational Research Group Memorandum No. 16, May 1950.

Ziegelmann, Fritz (1947). *The 352.Infanterie-Division: The Fighting from 23 June to 10 July 1944.* Foreign Military Studies B-439.

n.a. (1944). *German Defense in Hedgerow Terrain: Villiers-Fossard.* G-2, XIX Corps, July 1944.

n.a. (1946). *German Panzerfaust 100M.* Report 1983 of the AGF Infantry Board, Fort Benning, August 5, 1946.

n.a. (1951) *Present Status of the Tank Armor Program and Proposed Program for Development of Armor to Defeat HEAT and HEP Projectiles.* Technical Note 49, Ballistics Research Laboratory, Aberdeen Proving Ground, July 1951.

n.a. (2000). *The Use of Panzerfaust in the NW European Campaign, ORO Report No. 33*, in: Terry Copp, ed., *Montgomery's Scientists: Operational Research in Northwest Europe*. Wilfred Laurier University, Ontario.

TECHNICAL MANUALS

D 1862, 8.8cm R Werfer 43: Beschreibung, Bedienung und Behandlung, March 1, 1944.

D 1864/1, Panzerschreck 8.8cm R PzB 54 mit 8.8cm R PzBGr 4322, June 7, 1944.

D 1864/2, Panzerschreck 8.8cm R PzB 54 mit 8.8cm R PzBGr 4322, November 4, 1943.

D 1864/4, Panzerschreck 8.8cm R PzB 54 und 8.8cm R PzB 54/1 mit 8.8cm R PzBGr 4322 und R PzBGr 4992, December 1, 1944.

BOOKS

Berger, Hagen (2013). *Panzerknacker: Grenadiere im Nahkampf gegen Kolosse aus Stahl*. Munich: Verlag für Wehrwissenschaften.

Breyette,Thomas & R.J. Bender (2000). *Tank Killers: The History of the Tank Destruction Badge*. San Jose, CA: Bender.

Fedoseyev, Semyon (2014). *Istrebiteli tankov vtoroy mirovoy*. Moscow: Yauza.

de Vries, G. & B.J. Martens (2005). *German Anti-Tank Weapons*. Oosterbeek: Special Interest Publicaties.

n.a. (n.d). *Die Geschichte der 352.Infanterie-Division*. Kameradschaft.

ARTICLES

Erenfeicht, Leszek (2013). "Panzerfaust: A Fist to Knock Out Tanks," *Small Arms Review*, June 2013.

Lucy, Roger (2007). "Allied Trials of Measures to Counter Attacks by Panzerfaust," *AFV News*, September–December 2007.

Ochman, Marcin (2004). "Panzerfaust: Rozwój konstrukcji," *Nowa Technika Wojskowa*, No. 3.

Pawlas, Karl (1971). "Die Panzerfaust," *Waffen Revue*, Nr. 3, 1971.

Pawlas, Karl (1981). "Schürzen: zur Verstärkung der Panzerung," *Waffen Revue*, Nr. 40, 1981.

Pawlas, Karl (1998). "Die Panzerfaust 150," *Waffen Revue*, Nr. 111, 1998.

Spaulding, Donald (1984). "The Panzerfaust," *AFV News*, September–December 1984.

INDEX

References to illustrations are shown in **bold**.

antitank defenses (Ger), density of **63**, 74
antitank grenades (hand-emplaced/thrown) 74
   HH.3 8, 11–12, **12**, 18, 72, 74
   Panzerwurfmine-1 (leichte) 12, **13**
antitank grenades (rifle-fired) 12–13, 28, 29
antitank guns (Ger) 5, 10, 12, 53, 60, 68, 72
   allocation/density 6, 10–11, 52–53, 71
   tank kills 70, 73, 74
   types: PaK 36 5, 6, 10, 11, 13; PaK 38 5, 11;
     PaK 40 5, 11, 29, 52, 71
antitank mines (Ger) **63**, 70, 74: Teller 6
antitank rifles 4, 5, 11, 13, 36, 75
armor upgrade packages (US armies): FUSA 8, **8**, 27–
   28, 29, 32, **34**, 36–37, **38**, 45, 47–49, **49**, 75, **75**;
   NUSA **6**, 9, 31, **31**, 32–33, **33**, **49**, 77; SUSA 7, 9,
   33, **34**, 34, **35**, 36–37, 49–50, **49**; TUSA **1**, 9,
   33–34, **34**, 36
armored dvns (US) **6**, **7**, **8**, 9, 26–27, **28**, 30, 32, 34,
   38, 59, 60, 69, 70, **75**
   2d **6**, 32, 37, **38**, 57
   3d 9, 27, **28**, 37, **37**, 38, 57, 58, 59, 60, 70: CCA
     27, 58, 59, 60–61, 62, 65, 68, 69
   4th 34, 37
   6th 34, 37
   8th 30
   11th 34, **34**, 37
   12th 8, **8**, 34, **34**, 36, 37, 50, **75**
   14th **1**, 7, 34, **35**, 36, 37
armored groups (US) 26: 1st 9, 32, 36, 37, 50; 3d 9,
   28, 29; 7th 28; 11th 29
armored regts (US) **28**, 57: 32d 27, **28**, 58, 59, **70**;
   67th **6**
army groups (Ger) 52, **53**; (US) 29

Blanchard, Lt. Col. Elwyn W. 58, 68, **69**
British Army armor forces 5, 33, 38, 39
   tank losses 46, 71, 72, 73

camouflage net, use of **6**, 31, **31**, 32, **49**
Canadian Army armor forces 9, 33, 38, 39
   tank losses 46, 73
Cockefair, Lt. Col. Vincent E. 58, 65
   Cockefair (assault) Group 65, 68, **69**
Coolidge, Col. George W. 49, 50
concrete armor 8, **34**, 36–37, **38**, 45, 48, **49**, 75, **75**

Eastern Front, fighting on 5–6, **5**, 8, 11, 12, **15**, 16, 38,
   46, 51–52, 74, 75
engineer bns/squads (US) 27, 58

Fallschirm units 11, 53, 54, 56, 65, 68
Faustpatrone 8, 18, 20, 75: FP 1/FP 2 18, 20;
   F.P. 30/F.P. klein 30 20; FP 43 18, 20, **23**
Finnish Army forces **9**, **16**, 19, **21**
Flintkote Company 8, 29–30, **30**
fusilier bns (Ger) **53**, 56, **63**

German tanks 10, 32, 34, 36, 38, 44, 59, 74
Grenadier regts (Ger) 55, 56

HASAG 8, 9, 13–14, 18, 20, 22, 24, 38, 51
Hickey, Brig. Gen. Doyle O. 58, 68
HWA 11, 12, 13, 15, 16, 18, 20, 38

infantry bns/cos (Ger) 51, 55, 61; (US) 65
infantry dvns (Ger) 10, 51, 52, 54, 56: 58. 53; 189.
   55; 265. 54; 266. 54, 56; 275. 54; 277. 54; 343.
   56; 352. 54, 55–56, 57, 60, **69**, 70; 353. 56; (US)
   26: 29th 55, 56, 60, 62, 69; 30th 27
infantry regts (Ger) 20, 52–53, 54, 56, 71; (US) 60, 62
infantry–tank teams (US) 63, 65
Italy, fighting/tank losses in 14, 54, 73

jerrycans, use of 9, 27–28, 29, **30**

Kampfgruppen (battlegroups) 54, 56, **63**, 64, 65, 68,
   69, 70

Langweiler, Dr. Heinrich 18
layered armor 9, 32–33, **49**, 77

M1/M1A1 "bazooka" **9**, 13, 14, 20, 26, **32**, 36, 44,
   50, 76
M4(105mm) assault gun **36**
M4 medium tank 4, 7, 59
   armor protection/upgrades 28, 29, **30**, 31, **32**, 33,
     36, 44, 48
   combat use 56, **66–67**, **70**: losses 47, 56, **58**, 68,
     68, 74
   use in weapon evaluations 28, 29, 38, 50
M4A1(76mm) medium tank **28**, **37**, **47**, 59
M4A3 medium tank **6**, **73**
M4A3(76mm) medium tank **31**, 38
M4A3E8 medium tank 35
   armor upgrades 1, **8**, **30**, **33**, **34**, **35**, **75**
   combat losses 75
M5A1 light tank 29, 56, 58, 59, 70
M6A1 antitank rocket **14**
M72 LAW 44
M10 3in GMC tank destroyer 59, 68
maintenance bns/crews (US) 7, **8**, 34, 36
mesh aprons/skirts (Ger) 9, 32, 36, 38, 77; (US) 36
mesh screens (UK/Can) 39; (Sov) 9, 39

Normandy, fighting in
   bocage (hedgerow) terrain 26, 27, **28**, 56, **57**, 61–63,
     62, **66–67**, 70, **70**: German defense 54, 57, 60,
     61–62, 63; US offense 63: losses 54, 56, 71, 72

Orr, Lt. Col. William R. 58, 65
   Orr (assault) Group 65, **69**

Panzerfaust (Armor fist) 4, **5**, 7, 8, 13, 46, 51
   allocation/issue of 44, 51–52, 56, 61, 71, 72
   combat use/effectiveness 8, 9, **21**, 26, 27–28, 31, 39,
     39, 41, **41**, 42, 46, **46**, 47, 48, 51, 52, 54, 56, 60,
     63, 65, **66–67**, 70, 71–72, 73, **73**, 74: arming/
     aiming/firing of **9**, 22, 40–42, **41**, **45**, 46–47,
     46, **66–67**, **68**, 77; armor penetration by 39, **45**,
     47, 48, **75**; engagement ranges 9, 20, 22, 41, **41**,
     46, 70; Soviet use of 38, 75; tank/AFV kills 27,
     28, 29, 32, 34, 39, 46, 47, 54, 55, **58**, 59, 68, 70,
     71, 72, 73, 74, 75
   components/features **9**, 20, 22, 39, **40**, 41, **41**, 44,
     46, 47: shortcomings of 20, 22, 42, 44, 71
   field trials 51
   influence of 71
   munitions for 20, 22, 24, 26, 28, 44, **45**, **46**, 47, **68**,
     74, 77
   origins of 18, 20
   production 5, 9, 24, 26
   users **5**, 20, 54, 55, **55**
Panzerfaust 30 20, 40–42
Panzerfaust 30 (gross) **5**, **19**, 22, **23**, **25**, 26, 29, 48,
   57, **61**
Panzerfaust 30 (klein) **18**, 22, **23**, **25**, 26, 29, 39, 48
Panzerfaust 60 **4**, 22, **23**, 24, **25**, 26, 37, 39, 44, 46, 48, 50
Panzerfaust 100 9, 22, **23**, 24, **25**, 26, **26**, 30, 44–45,
   46–47, **46**, 48
Panzerfaust 150 **22**, **23**, 24, **25**, 76–77, **77**
Panzerfaust 250 **23**, 24, 76
Panzergrenadier bns/cos/dvns (Ger) 51, 53
Panzerjäger forces 52, 54, 74
Panzerschreck (Tank Terror) 4, 7, 8, **14**
   allocation/issue of 20, 52, 53, 56, 71, 72
   combat use/effectiveness 16, **16**, 20, 31, 32, 52, 53,
     53, 54, 56, 60, **63**, 71–72, 74: arming/aiming/

firing 14, 15, **15**, **16**, 17, 42–43; armor
   penetration by 29, 30, 44, 48, **75**; engagement
   ranges 15, 17, 43, **43**; impact of 26, 34, 71, 73;
   tank/AFV kills 8, 32, 34, 53, 54, 70, 71, 72, 73,
   74, 75
   components/features 8, **15**, 16, **16**, 17, 42–43, **43**:
     shortcomings 15, 16, 52, 71
   crews/gunners 8, **15**, 16, **16**, 53, **53**, 54
   evaluation/testing of 9, 28, 36, 52, 53
   munitions for 14, **14**, 15, 16–17, 29, 30, 44, 53
   production 15–16, 20
Panzervernichtungsabzeichen 8, 12, 53–54
Panzerzerstörer bns/cos/troops 52, 53
Patton, Gen. George S. **1**, 33, 34, 36
plastic armor 8, 29–30, **30**
Pool, CWO 2 Lafayette G. 47, 59, **59**
Puppchen 8, 13, 14–15, **14**, 53, 72

Raketenpanzerbüchse 13: RPzB 54 **4**, 8, 14, **15**, 17, **17**,
   20, **42**; RPzB 54/1 **4**, 9, 9, 17, **42**; RPzB 54/2 17
Raketenpanzerbüchse-Granate: RPzBGr 4312 13, 14, 15;
   RPzBGr 4322 14, **14**, 17; RPzBGr 4992
   Kurzbrenner 16–17
Red Army forces 38, 39, **39**, 52, 75
   encounters with *Panzerfäuste* 6, 12, 52: counter-
     screens, use of 9, 39, **39**; tank/AFV losses 39,
     74–75
   tanks 5, 6, 10, 11, 12, **39**, 75
Richardson, Lt. Col. Walter B. 58, **69**, 70
Russell, Lt. Col. Carlton P. 58, **69**

sandbag armor 33, 39, 50
   density/weight of 33, **49**, 75
   effectiveness of 37, 47–50
   evaluation/testing of 9, 38, 45, 49–50
   penetration of 48–49, 50
   use of **1**, 6, 7, 8, 9, 27–28, **28**, 29, 30, 31, **31**, 32,
     33, **35**, 36, **47**, **49**
shaped-charge (warhead) technology 6–7, 11–12, 24,
   44, 47, 48, **68**, 76–77
spaced armor 29, 39, 50, **50**, 77
spike armor 27, 29, 31, 39
steel cages, use of **7**, **33**, **35**, 36, 50

tank bns (US) 29, 58: 18th **30**; 23d 36; 25th **35**, 49;
   48th 49; 191st **33**; 709th 37; 712th 29; 735th 29;
   741st 28–29; 743d 27–28, **47**, **73**; 744th 28;
   747th 31, 56, **58**, 60, 62; 749th 29; 759th 28, 29;
   separate bns (US) 26, 27–28, 32, 36, 37–38
tank cos (US) 58, **58**, 65
tank-destroyer bns/platoons (US) 58, 63, 68
tank tracks, use of **49**
task forces (US) 58, 68, 69, **70**: TF X 58, 59, 64–65,
   68, 69, **69**, 70, **70**; TF Y 59, 65, 68, **69**; TF Z 59,
   65, 68, 69
track blocks/links, use of **6**, **30**, **31**, 32, 33, 38

Villers-Fossard (salient), battle of 8, 28, 55–62, **63**,
   64–65, **66–67**, 68–69, **69**, 70, **70**: *Panzerfaust* tank
   kills 27, **58**, 71; *Panzerschreck* tank kills 71; tank
   losses 27, **58**, 59, 68, **68**, 69, 70, 71

WASAG 12–13, 13–14, 20
Whitlaw, Lt. Col. Nathaniel O. 58, 65, 68
   Whitlaw (assault) Group 65, 68, **69**, 70
wire mesh, use of 37, **49**

Zubrod, Leutnant Heinrich 54, 55, **55**